WIT
SWF
MAL
BNHM
CGSL
HAT
KEL
SIL
SMST
WIB
MOB

6|93

BLACKWATER MEN

By
Arthur and Michael Emmett

SEAX BOOKS
ELSENHAM, BISHOP'S STORTFORD

First published by Seax Books 1992

MLP Ltd, Market Link House, Elsenham, Bishop's Stortford, Herts CM22 6DY

Illustrations: Maps and drawings by Julie Sinclair
Photographs by Arthur and Michael Emmett or by kind permission of their friends.
The photographs of Flushing (pages 22/23) and Boulogne (pages 64/65) courtesy of the
Trustees of the Imperial War Museum, London

ISBN 870112 17 2

Printed by The Bath Press, Bath

FL92109

FOREWORD

This book is a fascinating, inspiring and sometimes humbling story of a man who was determined to earn his living - and his freedom - on the sea, and of others who were born into a tight knit community of watermen.

As a sailor with a love of adventure, I can sympathise with Arthur Emmett, faced with a humdrum life once the war was over unless he took his destiny into his own hands. He did just that and managed to earn a living from the sea and the boat he loved - a love he passed on to his son.

I can admire, too, the men of the River Blackwater who were born to fish and sail and, despite the hardships, firmly maintained their traditions continuing to prefer sail without engines long after other fishing communities had become completely motorised.

Michael Emmett tells the story of these people with affection and understanding, for he became one of them when his father married into the local community. Michael was taught their skill and their secrets but keeps enough of an outsider's perspective to admire their vast store of knowledge passed from generation to generation - a knowledge that was so appreciated by the 'gentlemen' yachtsmen of pre-war years who chose these men to become their professional crews.

The spirit of adventure that has inspired sailors for generations will continue and there will always be new challenges. Those of us who have faced our own trials, enjoy and appreciate the stories of those who went before us. Those who are happy to stay on the shore and watch, will also appreciate the breath of sea air that comes from every page of this book.

Chay Blyth CBE BEM

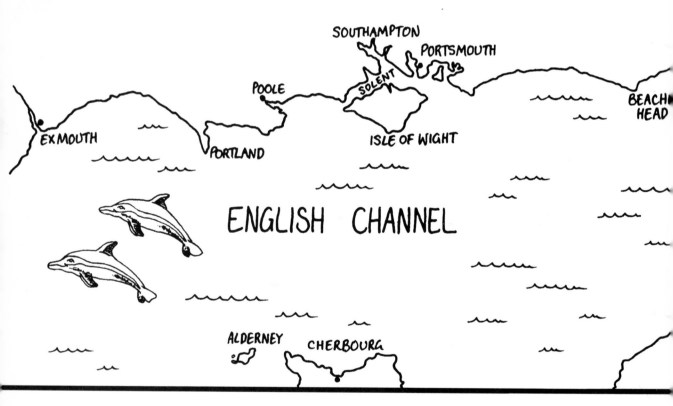

ENGLAND

RIVER BLACKWATER

LONDON

SOUTHAMPTON

PORTSMOUTH

POOLE

SOLENT

BEACHY HEAD

EXMOUTH

PORTLAND

ISLE OF WIGHT

ENGLISH CHANNEL

ALDERNEY

CHERBOURG

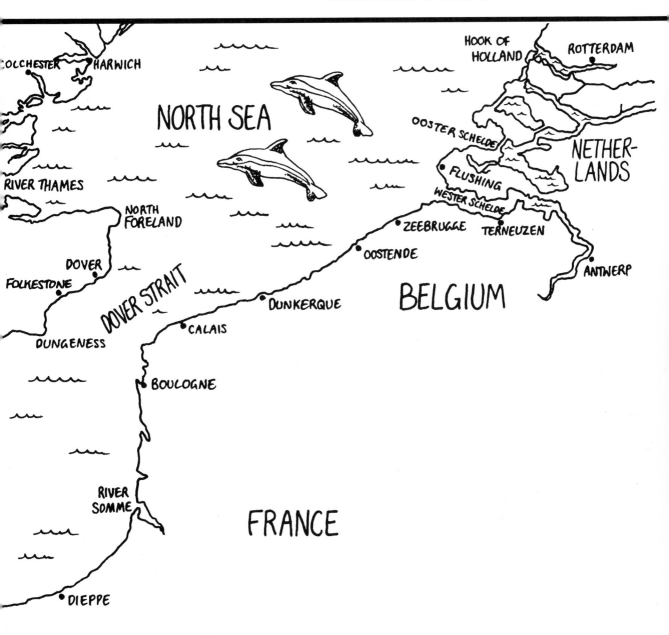

COLCHESTER   HARWICH

NORTH SEA

RIVER THAMES

NORTH FORELAND

DOVER

FOLKESTONE

DUNGENESS

DOVER STRAIT

CALAIS

BOULOGNE

RIVER SOMME

DIEPPE

FRANCE

DUNKERQUE

OOSTENDE

ZEEBRUGGE

HOOK OF HOLLAND

ROTTERDAM

OOSTER SCHELDE

FLUSHING

WESTER SCHELDE

TERNEUZEN

ANTWERP

NETHER-LANDS

BELGIUM

This map shows the areas of the North Sea and English Channel where Topsy sailed in the years immediately after the war.
Overleaf: a detailed map of the Essex estuaries of the Blackwater, Colne and Crouch

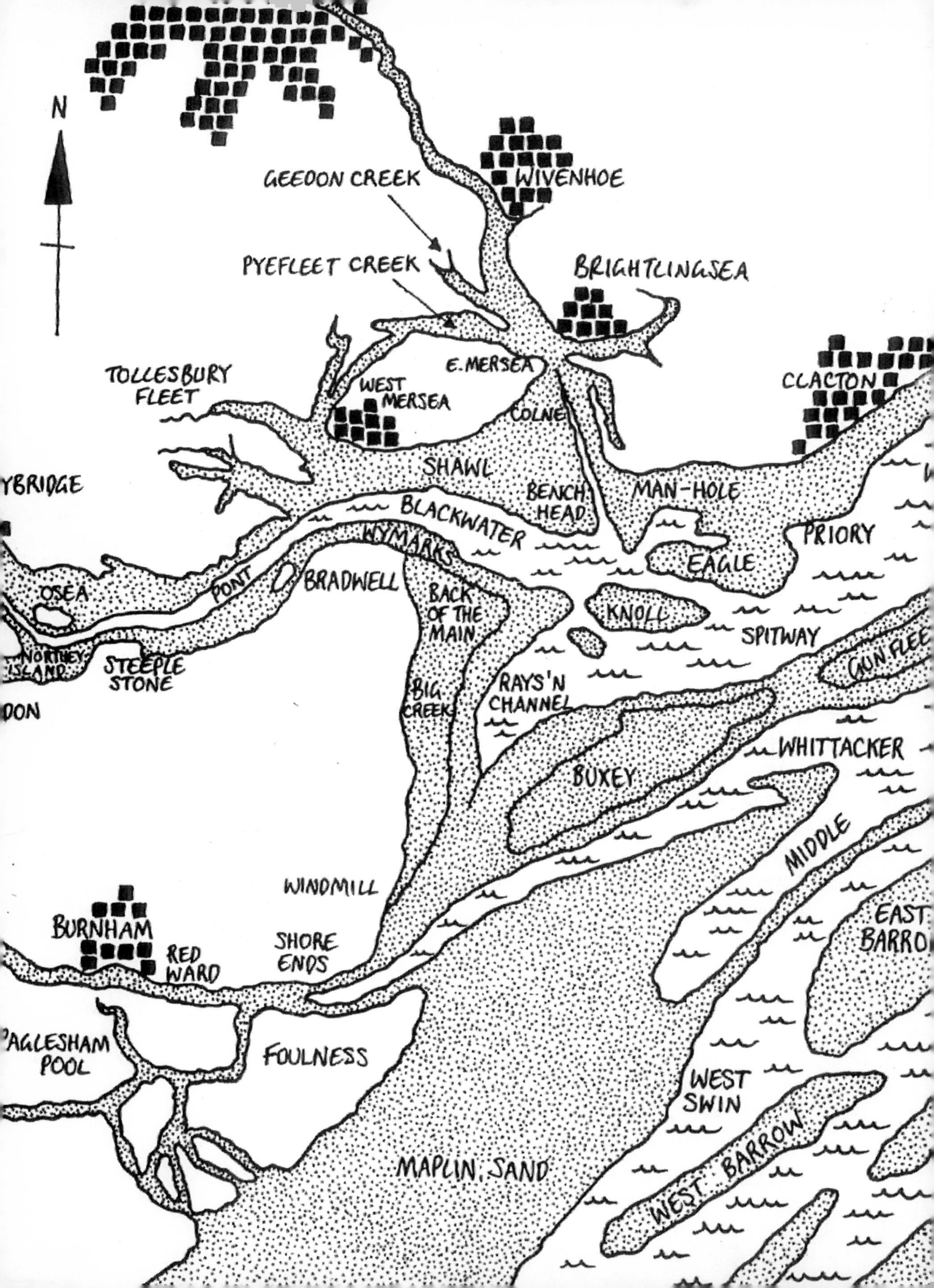

N

GEEDON CREEK

WIVENHOE

PYEFLEET CREEK

BRIGHTLINGSEA

TOLLESBURY
FLEET

E. MERSEA

WEST
MERSEA

CLACTON

COLNE

SHAWL

YBRIDGE

BENCH
HEAD

MAN-HOLE

BLACKWATER

PRIORY

WYMARKS

EAGLE

PONT

BRADWELL

BACK
OF THE
MAIN

KNOLL

SPITWAY

OSEA

GUN FLEE

NORTHEY
ISLAND

STEEPLE
STONE

BIG
CREEK

RAYS'N
CHANNEL

DON

WHITTACKER

BUXEY

MIDDLE

WINDMILL

BURNHAM

RED
WARD

SHORE
ENDS

EAST
BARRO

'AGLESHAM
POOL

FOULNESS

WEST
SWIN

MAPLIN SAND

WEST BARROW

CONTENTS

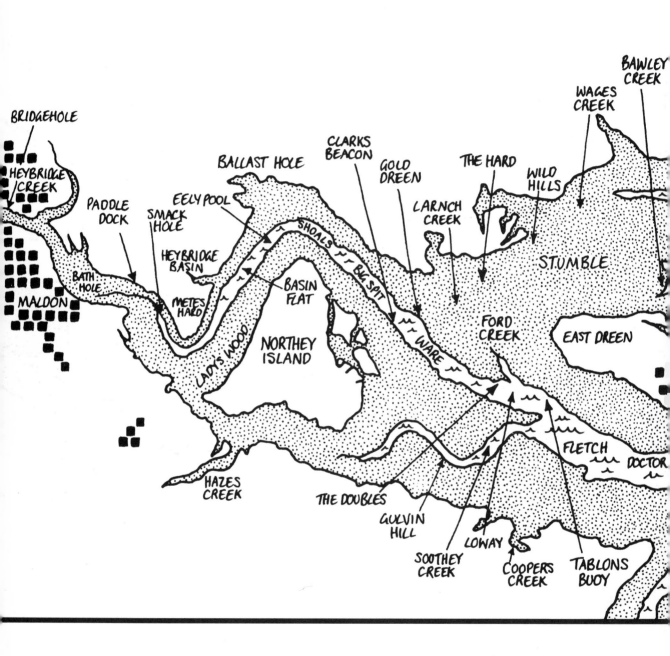

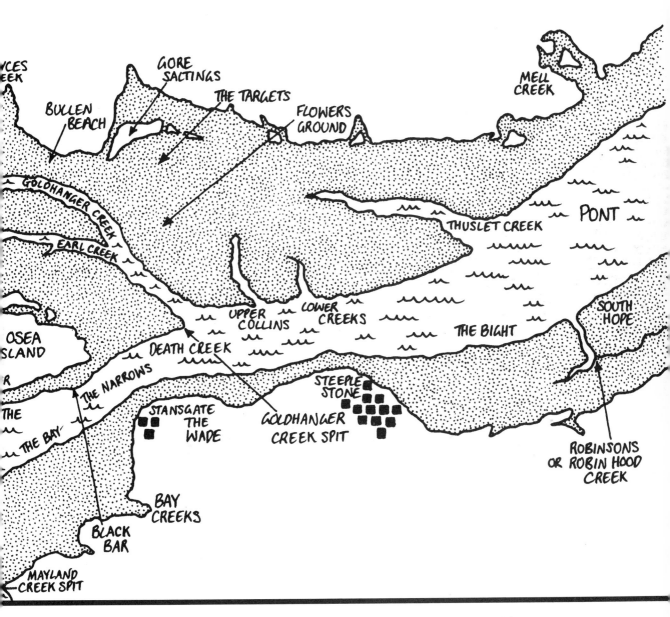

The River Blackwater represented the entire world to some of the old hands as they seldom, if ever, went anywhere else, on land or sea. Probably because of this, nearly every inch of mud and every tiny trickle of water had a name to define it

To Sue who inspired me to write this book and to Geraldine
Courtney for her hours of dedication

I would also like to acknowledge the help I have received
from Doug Pitt, Ted Pitt, Cecil Stebbings, Cecil Wright,
Gerald Wright, 'Butts' Yardley and 'King' Wright, in my
opinion the best fisherman in Maldon and the man who taught
me the greater part of what I have learned.

Thanks, too, to everyone who has helped me on this venture in
any way

INTRODUCTION

The outskirts of Maldon, Essex, are much the same as any other small town in southern England these days - new roads, roundabouts and small industrial estates. The centre of the town, though, retains that special charm that only water and boats can bring. A breath of fresh air blows up from the Hythe quay, bringing with it a hint of adventure, freedom and faraway places. But there is unlikely to be a smell of fish on the air now, for the Maldon fishing industry has disappeared.

The fishing smacks that once lined the Bath Wall have gone, or they have been restored for pleasure and to race by wooden boat enthusiasts. The commercial use of the Thames barges which add so much to the atmosphere of The Hythe today is limited to charter work.

This book charts that change from the days when the longshoremen of Maldon earned their living from the river and the majestic barges - more attractive to look at than to sail and live in - made Maldon a thriving port despite its position well up river. It is a story of adventure, too, and of two men's love of the water and sail.

Arthur Emmett came to Maldon after the war to try to earn a living chartering his yacht, long before the romance of traditional craft was generally recognised. Most of the passengers he took to Belgium, Holland and France were simply looking for a way to reach the continent in those early post-war years when the seas were still heavily mined and there was no such thing as cross channel ferries leaving every hour.

If there had been a more modern and more comfortable alternative to sailing in *Topsy*, they would have taken it.

Arthur Emmett and *Topsy* were before their time and the chartering business lasted only a few years. After a spell as the landlord of The Ship in Market Hill, Maldon, Arthur Emmett returned to sea in the mid-Fifties when he became a Dover pilot. *Topsy* was finally broken up and became a houseboat.

Arthur Emmett had been born in Brentford in 1907 and before the war he ran a garage, occasionally raced at Brooklands and enjoyed a successful secondary career as an operatic tenor, doing dubbing work for films and singing as a guest artist with various operatic societies. He knew Maldon in those days and brought his two yachts, *Topsy* and *Iolanthe*, to the town as early as 1927 when he became a founder member of the Maldon Little Ship Club. His own father had spent part of his childhood days in Maldon and had been apprenticed at Walter Cook and Sons boatyard on The Hythe - an apprenticeship that lasted for just two hours, so the story goes. He decided that any job that involved taking your jacket off was not worth doing, so he left for Southampton where a land deal started him on the road to success.

Iolanthe was taken for war service by the Admiralty but Arthur Emmett came back to Maldon and *Topsy* after the war and the first volume of this book is the story of his sailing adventures in the late 1940s.

A generation on, Arthur's son Michael Emmett can still be found on The Hythe chartering his own traditionally built *Ostrea Rose*, but the passengers who sail with him come through choice, not necessity. They, like him, are held by the spell of water and traditional sail.

But the simple fact that Michael Emmett charters his boat just as his father did before him, hides a complex tale of changing times, attitudes and economics. Michael's own story, told in volume two, is the story of Maldon's watermen through the century, a celebration and a tribute to their skills.

He was born into this world of watermen that his father had come to know and respect. Perhaps it is this unique inheritance of his father's respect for the community as an outsider and his grandmother's deep involvement in the traditions handed down through generations of smacksmen, along with their boats, that has given Michael an appreciation of the way of life of a community which has virtually disappeared.

Most of the old fishing families have now left to find work on shore, but Michael Emmett remains at The Hythe, one of the few who can make the link between Maldon's commercial and pleasure sailing days.

"The water is like a magnet," he admits. "I can't stay away from it for long."

Michael Emmett can be contacted through Traditional Charter, 71 Gloucester Avenue, Chelmsford, Essex CM2 9DR.

BLACKWATER MEN

VOLUME ONE

By Arthur Emmett

OPERATION CIVVY STREET

As the train pulled out of Lowestoft Station on that Saturday morning in October 1945 when I received my discharge from the Royal Navy, I was filled with mixed feelings, for I felt that I was speeding away for ever from a life that had become a part of me, and that I was rushing towards one that would be new and very dull in the future.

True, I had studied the little booklet taking in every angle of rehabilitation which had been supplied to me, as it had to thousands of other men and women at that time in the same position as myself. But my careful study of this book of instructions had left me cold. Everything had been worked out so wonderfully that it gave me the impression that there must be a snag somewhere.

To leave a life crammed full of adventure, interest, and uncertainty to join millions of others in a life of certainty, social security and monotony, simply did not excite me in the least. An unpatriotic way of thinking? No, I don't think so, for I felt I would just be a very small square peg in a large round hole and, therefore, pretty useless.

I was free of the well-ordered routine of the Royal Navy which had been my lot since the war started and, being without home or dependents, I was free to please myself how and where I lived. I did not have a clue what I would do after my de-mob leave had expired, but firstly I was journeying to Maldon in Essex, where my ketch, *Topsy,* had survived the war lying in the mud dock behind Charley Barker's boat yard at the Downs.

I arrived in Maldon and was greeted by Charley Barker himself. We walked down his yard to have a look at the yacht. I was devastated by my first glance at the old lady, remembering how spick and span she had looked when I left her in 1939. Was this dilapidated hulk my *Topsy*? I could see that she was by her line, but her appearance was shocking. Her deck was green, paintwork had peeled from her sides and, long ago, all varnished wood had turned black.

Charley assured me that she was in fine condition and on going aboard to inspect her I found that she had really weathered the war years very well. *Topsy* had been put in her berth on a very high spring tide as the entrance of the dock had less water than the dock itself. Inside the dock, the ketch could float on high water spring tides, but without an abnormally high tide it was impossible to get her out, short of digging a channel through the mud astern of her.

It was because of this that *Topsy* was never taken by the Admiralty as so many other boats were, nor was it necessary to remove a plank from above her water line in order to immobilise her. On two occasions the Admiralty inspected the yacht, but as they could not move her out of the dock either time, they decided that nobody else could do so either and so they left her there. I have no idea why they did not commandeer the inside lead ballast for the war effort but it was my good fortune that it was still on board when I returned.

The bottom of the yacht, when we examined it later, was found to be in splendid condition. There is no worm in the mud there and because of the dampness of the mud and the fact that the bottom was wetted with each tide, I found that she was tight as a drum as far as the waterline and only needed a scrub and a repaint.

I am not a believer in hauling yachts out of the water for long periods and the condition of some of the yachts that have been hauled out in the yards at Maldon rather supports my belief. I looked at several and found that in some cases you could slide a pencil through between their planks.

Going below deck, I found that the once beautifully French polished saloon looked very drab indeed as Charley had left the yacht open to the air throughout the war. Although it certainly saved dry rot from forming, it allowed the weather to take the wonderful finish off the woodwork. I was delighted later when the hardwood came up as good as new after washing down and varnishing.

Every bit of paintwork inside and out had to be burned off. It took a full three weeks to scrape the cabin trunk and hatches - a very tedious job although I was never short of helpers, for many lads on their de-mob leave would come aboard for something to do. The top sides and the deck required recaulking and this work was later carried out by Cook and Son, as Charley was by then overrun with work and could not undertake to do it.

I well remember one awful night I spent aboard during torrential rain. Sleep was impossible and I could find nowhere below deck where the rain did not wet. Nevertheless for all that, the yacht was sound, which is more than many unfortunate owners could say about their own yachts after the war had finished. There was nothing wrong with *Topsy* that a little hard work could not put right and all the spars and gear, which had been ashore, were in excellent condition.

Topsy is one of the old type gaff rigged yachts built on the lines of a fishing smack. She looks rather like a slender edition of a Brixham mule. Her deck length is 52 feet, with a beam of 12 feet 9 inches and draught of 5 feet 6 inches. In a really long sea she is a grand sea boat. She is very stiff and, like other yachts of her age, she has the ability to heave-to without trouble and can then be left unattended in almost anything - within reason.

She was built in 1911 by the original Aldous Yard at Brightlingsea but she has a strange history of alteration and construction. For years she was rigged as a cutter and had no engine. Later a small engine was fitted and in 1920 she was almost completely rebuilt, lengthened by 12 feet in the centre, and altered into a yawl. Later she assumed the guise of a 'half-sprit' and had a mainsail that brailed up. Finally, she was altered into a ketch with a Bermudan mizzen sail In her construction, only the best selected hardwoods were used. Her timbers are of English oak, all panelling and hatches are teak, with pitch pine planking, Koen pine decks and pitch pine masts. The straight keel is lead as is the inside ballast.

The regular changes to the yacht gave her her name - like Topsy she just grow'd.

There is a surprising amount of room down below as she is all boat, sleeping four in the forecastle, two in the saloon where the bunks hinge down from above the settees, two in the sleeping cabin and one in the cabin aft. It once had two bunks aft, but I removed one to fit a coal range and a water tank.

Topsy - built at Brightlingsea in 1911

My lunch hours and evenings were spent at the top of the town with the lads who were just out of the services like myself, and I renewed the acquaintance of many old friends and made scores of new ones. Our usual places to foregather were the King's Head, then kept by that most genial of mine hosts, Corny, and at the Blue Boar. Being back in Maldon was like coming home to me, for nowhere else had I seen a town where so little change had taken place, or where people had aged or altered so little.

Maldon is odd. There is something about it, but if you were asked to define what this 'something' or attraction was, you would find yourself unable to do so. In actual fact, the town is neither one thing or the other. It is not seaside, nor is it just country. It is the port of Maldon, but it is situated twelve miles up the River Blackwater where the reaches dry out above Osea Island. It is a fair sized town, but it peters out at the bottom of the High Street to become an old-fashioned fishing village, with the 17 or so fishing boats taking the ground at low water off the Bath Wall.

Here the local fishermen like to gather when off work, to chat and argue in their broad Essex tongues about anything or nothing. Here, also, age has stood still and several grand old men who have spent their lives upon the waters in sailing coasters, fishing smacks and barges, wear their three-score years and ten more lightly than many a townsman of middle age.

At the time of writing, the old fishermen Ernie and Wal Pitt are still earning their living down river and out in the estuary along the Knoll and Raysand Channels in their fast little sailing smack, *Polly*, which has never had an engine - and while Wal and Ernie are alive it never will. Although they work their fish trawl by hand, Ernie appears to thrive on his physically hard life in spite of his 75 years. Wal, his brother and mate, follows him equally actively with 67 years to his credit. 'Little Owd Polly', which Ernie assures me talks to him, is somewhere near to Wal's age. They are a really splendid combination and not one of them could exist without the other two.

When winkling time comes round, and at the time when the tides are ebbing in the morning and flooding in the afternoon, these two elderly gentlemen amaze me by leaving home at 4 in the morning - more often than not on a bitterly raw cold day - each rowing a duck punt to go down river to pick up a bushel of winkles each. They then row back on the next flood tide. To the layman this may read as not amounting to very much but anyone who has tried even walking through the mud of the Blackwater can really appreciate the labour involved.

Let them try wearing wooden mud shoes, or splatches as they are called, and attempt to find and gather a bushel of winkles before the next tide floods once more across the mud. Having gathered what really amounts to three quarters of a hundred weight of winkles, let them attempt to carry the sack across the mud to the punts, to really learn what hard work and back ache can mean.

The duck punts are specially designed to float in very shallow water and, with their flat bottoms, they are ideal for drawing across the soft mud of our east coast estuaries

One day, I went down river with Ernie and Wal and tried winkling, with the result that, although I am only 40 years old, Wal picked up twice as many winkles as I did and took everything in his stride. He carried on with no more concern than if he was picking flowers in a garden, whilst I suffered from back ache and aching leg muscles for the next two days. Every man to his job. I suppose it is a case of 'it's not what you do, but the way that you do it.'

I find the broad Essex dialect of the local fishermen a sheer delight and they employ many odd expressions and words. They never speak of their boats as having been cleaned but as having 'clent' them. To go over the side when swimming is to 'dove' overboard, with the first vowel well and truly stressed. A large sail area will bring the comment that 'that little owd bot has a rare mainsil.' Everything is spoken of as 'little owd' and it sounds very strange when they apply the term to a boy of four or to a puppy. When a boat becomes water-borne she is said to 'fleet' and to return home up the river on the tide with no engine and no wind is to 'drive up'.

Topsy's war berth with Charley Barker aboard

There is always interest at the riverside in Maldon, especially if you are accepted by the locals, although it does appear that you are still a foreigner unless you are Maldon born or can prove residence in the district for well over 25 years.

In the Jolly Sailor or the Queen's Head, Maldon's two waterside pubs, topics of 40 years ago are still talked over and argued about with as much enthusiasm as are present day ones, such as the football the Swifts played at Heybridge last Saturday.

This was the atmosphere I chose to transport me from the war back to peacetime routine.

It very nearly did make me feel that I was once again back to the summers I spent around Maldon before the war came to change the face of everything; but I received a rude awakening when I started to refit the yacht. It was sheer misery getting permits, for this, that and the other, and

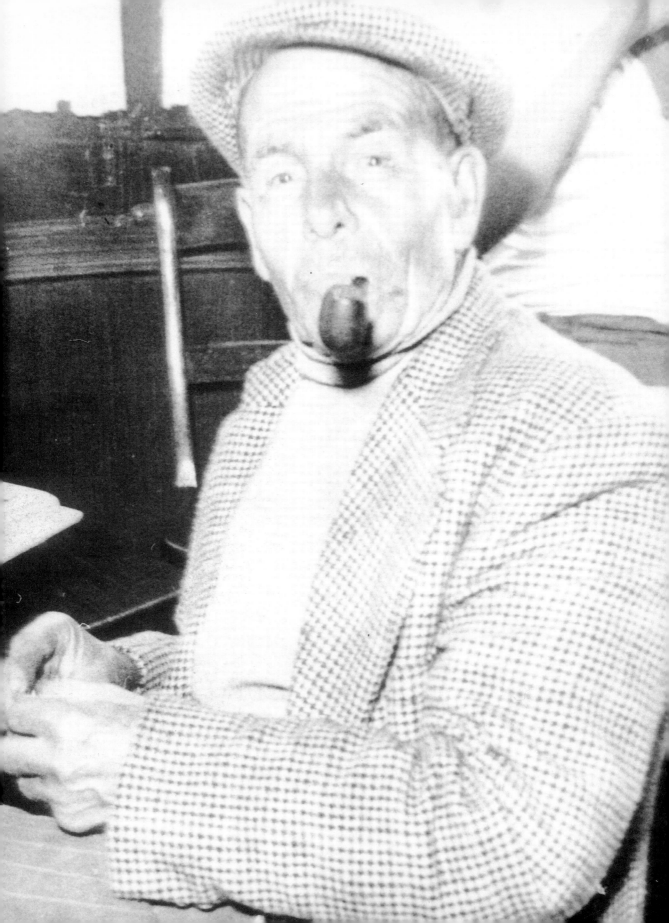

I found it was more difficult to purchase a small piece of timber than it once was to get a boat built. Probably the most difficult task of all - and the one with the greatest delay - was to obtain an allocation of petrol for the B2 Kelvin engine and for the charging plant. When I did receive an allocation it was too small to be of any real use.

The re-fitting of the *Topsy* was well under way when romance came along, fostered by an illness. Through Ernie and Wal Pitt I had come to know their niece, Olive, who at that time was about 17 years old.

One day, Olive wondered why she had not seen me around for a day or two and walked down to the yacht to find a reason. There she discovered me lying collapsed in my bunk, unable to fend for myself. She immediately ran for her mother who sent for a car and had me moved to her house. Olive's mother Agnes, or Aggie as she is generally called, had lost her husband in very tragic circumstances about a year before

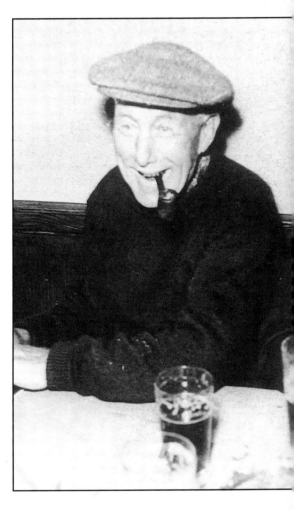

The doctor was called and I was diagnosed as having a severe attack of quinzies. During the time I was recovering, I received the finest attention possible. Aggie was insistent that I must never again live aboard *Topsy* alone, so from then on I stayed on as a lodger and one of the family at her home. Without any effort on my part, one of my major problems had been solved for me. I had found a home.

And my new home led me to my wife. The friendship that had developed with Olive blossomed under her mother's roof and we were to be married four years later - in 1949.

I had been involved with boats and the sea at Maldon in pre-war years and Maldon was always part of me, but to the real townsfolk I would remain an interloper, however friendly they might be to a fellow waterman. But marriage made me a part of the community, gave me relatives and roots in a delightful part of the world.

The next problem was to find a job. What should I do? I could sell the yacht and invest the money in a business ashore, but that was out of the question at the time because small businesses were very much sought af-

Ernie Pitt (opposite page) and Wal Pitt (above)

ter and were fetching prices that were out of all reason. Should I go back to sea? Yes, that was more like it - and why not in *Topsy*. Perhaps I could make her pay for herself and bring me a living, too. I decided to have a shot at that and, gamble or not, I set about doing it. I could carry passengers, fish, do day trips down river as far as Brightlingsea, take weekly or longer cruises home or abroad and act as a freelance skipper or runner skipper on other people's boats in between bookings - always providing I found customers.

The only advertising that I did was to mingle with everyone and to put up a trade card and photograph of *Topsy* in the King's Head and Jolly Sailor. But through this I did find customers which at least was a start. I had no illusions about my social standing among the 'pukka' yachtsmen. There was no question about it, I would be an outcast. It was just one of those things that is not done - fancy using a yacht for business!

I had already thought this one through and had come to the conclusion that the line between openly using your own yacht for business and taking paying guests or chartering the boat is very thin indeed, but in the first case you are an unspeakable cad and not recognised as a yachtsman anyway, while if you take guests who pay their way or charter you can still hold your yachting standing.

As I could see it, the thin line was between advertising for guests you have never previously met and saying to someone you vaguely know while drinking together in a cocktail bar: "I say, old chap, I would be awfully bucked to have your company on a cruise in my motor yacht to Deauville next month. Should be a topping do, you know. It won't cost you much - just your own expenses, old boy, something around the £50 mark. Let me know if you can make it and give me a ring about Thursday."

Those who can and do afford to run a large yacht, I exclude from these comments, but I see no reason for the airs assumed by the types who profess not to be using their yachts for commercial purposes but still ensure that their guests pay for their upkeep and running expenses. There is all the difference in the world between this type of yachtsman, whom I have met ashore in the French ports, parading in white flannels and white topped cap displaying lily white hands, and the real yachting enthusiast, tired, wet and hungry when making a passage for the sheer joy of the thing, and the pleasure and skill of sailing. He will muck in with his friends to finance a trip that might otherwise be beyond his means. For the yachtsman of the ocean racing fraternity, I have the greatest admiration.

I could no longer be called a yachtsman because, in the future, getting from A to B in the shortest possible time would be my first consideration. Like all the old type straight-keeled and straight-stem yachts, *Topsy* is slow to windward, but whereas in the past I took pleasure in mixing that bit of rough with the smooth of a glorious dash with a stiff reaching wind, I would now have to use my engine whenever I found that I was wasting time.

Reaching is the old yacht's best point of sailing when, with the wind blowing from abeam, all the sails draw at their maximum efficiency.

No longer would I sail, or drift when there was no wind, for pleasure. *Topsy* would now be a working boat and undoubtedly would look like one before the season finished.

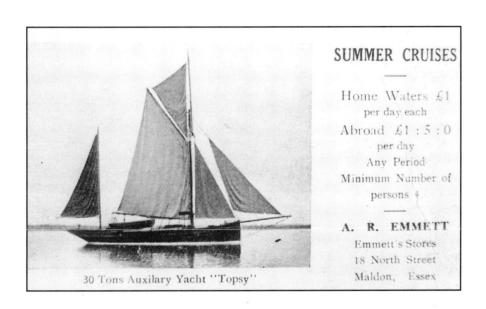

30 Tons Auxilary Yacht "Topsy"

SUMMER CRUISES

Home Waters £1
per day each
Abroad £1 : 5 : 0
per day
Any Period
Minimum Number of
persons 4

A. R. EMMETT
Emmett's Stores
18 North Street
Maldon, Essex

READY FOR SEA - AT LAST

*T*opsy was ready at last. What a glorious feeling it was to take her to sea for the first time since before the war! The month of March 1946 brought a series of gales and high winds, but the last day of the month dawned with every promise of a good trial trip.

Reg Markham had just left the Navy and came to help me, and, with Aggie, her baby, Ann, Olive and her girlfriend, Jean Gibson, we started off in grand style with the local fishermen shaking their heads and predicting that we would drown ourselves as it was too early in the season for coasting.

With a moderate south westerly wind we sailed out to the Swin Spitway, arriving there with just enough water left to float us through, but we had to use the engine to be able to do it in time over the ebb. At the Whittaker Bell buoy we tried to set the topsail and then trouble started and hard work began.

When I re-rigged after the war I could only replace worn out Italian hemp and manila with that wretched makeshift, sisal. I find that it is a very hard rope to handle until it is nearly worn out. As a topsail sheet it was a total wash-out as it preferred to tie itself into innumerable figures of eight and - even worse - formed a half-hitch around the gaff end which meant lowering the mainsail to clear it. Hard work for only two hands.

Speaking of hands reminds me of the agony I suffered on that trip with my hands and fingers. I would never have believed that my hands could have grown so soft while I was in the Navy, but I had literally lost the skin off them handling ropes on this first journey and they were almost unusable by the time we anchored in Dover.

We anchored in shore opposite the wreck of the destroyer *Codrington* which I saw bombed and sunk in 1940. She was lost in the submarine basin at the eastern side of the harbour with, fortunately, only a small number of casualties, but her wreck was lifted and stranded on the beach for breaking up.

We landed on the beach and took the dinghy's anchor on a long rope to above high water mark. Ashore, many old memories of the Dover Patrol were revived for Reg and myself, and I was very lucky in running into some of my brother officers - Lieutenant Bradshaw, Lt Commander Mowbry and Lieutenant Lowe. Max Lowe commanded the minesweeping trawler, HMS. *Alexandrite*, when I commanded HMS *Ronso*, of the same breed, and we had a great deal to say to each other. Another old friend we spent the evening with was John Mead who ran the Dover Club throughout the war in spite of anything Gerry dropped or slung across the Channel.

The crew of HMS Ronso in 1942 with the author front row left

After a splendid evening and a good dinner in The Crypt, we made for the dinghy to discover that some imp of Satan had thrown our anchor as far off shore at low water as he could make it go, and that we were marooned on the beach with the boat far out of reach. As an end to a perfect day, we waited shivering on the beach until 3 am before we could get aboard!

On our return trip, *Topsy's* entry into the port of her birth was spectacular, but it was also a fine example of how a yacht should not be managed. Our meagre ration of petrol had disappeared into the old Kelvin engine, hungry some days before, so we were forced to sail in. Being as short-handed as we were, I should have anchored in the River Colne and used the dinghy to get ashore, but we worked out exactly what we would do and proceeded to carry out our plan.

The mainsail was lowered at the mouth of Brightlingsea Creek and under headsails only we sailed in with a fair tide at half flood. We had no room to put about, so the jib was stowed when we were halfway in and the foresail was dropped at the precise moment to leave us sufficient steerage way to reach the fishing boat anchorage off the Stone at St Osyth. Everything worked to plan and the anchor cable was flaked out over the winding

Overleaf: Maldon

lass. The anchor *should* have dragged on the river, *Topsy should* have slowed down, the anchor with more cable paid out *should* have dug in, and *Topsy should* have swung head to tide. But none of these things happened.

The yacht went careering on among all the small boats at anchor and on moorings. We hurt none and dodged many, but one boat followed us with the tenacity of a hound on the scent for we had lifted its moorings. We carried it with us to where we piled nicely on the mud below the saltings. A local boatman assisted us to kedge off and towed us to a vacant harbour board buoy.

A few minutes later a very irate harbour master came alongside in his motor launch and, not very politely, told me what he thought of me - especially as the moorings we had lifted were his. I explained to him how our anchor had never left the bows but had hooked itself up on the bob-stay of the bowsprit, and asked him aboard to have a pineapple rum, which was all that I had in the way of liquid refreshment. That type of rum must be very potent stuff for we settled our differences easily over a couple of tots, and Harold Day, the harbour master, and I have been very good friends ever since.

With women aboard ship you never know what to expect. Aggie shook me to the core on the morning of the second day of our trip by asking me where she could get more fresh water. In one day the ladies had emptied my main fresh water tank which held sufficient for a week. They must have used water by the bucketful.

Olive, a seaman's daughter who was afloat before she was old enough to realise it, was so seasick she passed right out, while little Ann thought it was all good fun. Jean astonished us. She had never been aboard a boat in her life before, yet she could stick it out in the forecastle holding a kettle onto the Calor gas stove, while the yacht was punching into a head sea.

The run up to Maldon on the following morning completed our trial run.

* * * * * * * *

After several local runs, I signed on two lads who were the sons of local fishermen for *Topsy's* first trip abroad. Allan Wright was tall with dark hair and he was strong and cheeky, whilst Phil Bond, although as dark, was of slighter build.

With the two boys as crew we sailed to Dover to meet our five guest passengers who arrived with enough suitcases to carry all the clothes they would have needed for a six month's cruise in a luxury liner. I was faced with the problem of where to stow them after their contents had been placed in the various lockers, drawers and cupboards below deck. In the end I lashed them in a row under a tarpaulin on the cabin top.

All that morning a thunderstorm hung about the Dover area and the rain fell in sheets, but with the passing of the storm we were left with flat calm and sunshine when we motored out in the afternoon.

One of the passengers, Mr B, took the wheel and everybody was happy joking and lolling about on the deck. But they were to be disillusioned very soon, I'm afraid, because there is a lot more to yachting than sunshine, flat calms and leisure to sunbathe.

At the North West Goodwin buoy a fog descended and soon we were shivering with the cold as we groped our way around the North Goodwin Sands, a place that three years of minesweeping night and day had taught me to treat with the utmost respect. Passing the North Goodwin Light Vessel whose fog-signal boomed away close to us, we set a course for the South Falls bell buoy where, happily, a fine south west wind sprang up and the fog disappeared as if by magic. We set the mainsail, foresail and jib, and, with the engine silent, we were soon cracking along at a steady average of 6.5 knots.

After the war, the menace of mines was still a very real danger and would remain so for years to come, so we were sailing along the NF, or North Foreland to Flushing swept channel route, which had been cleared of all mines to a width of one mile. *Topsy* is of wooden construction and so she would not activate a magnetic mine while her shallow draught could take her safely over any moored mines. But, all the same, my wartime experience of these abomina-

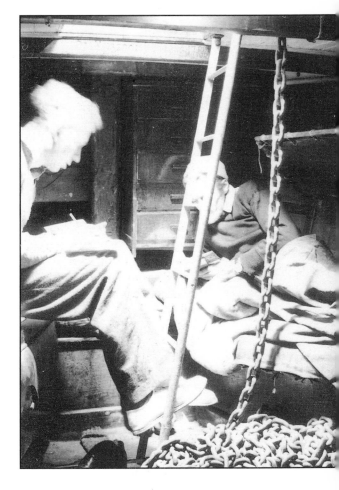

Topsy's forecastle - with room to sleep four

tions has always kept me to the swept channels even when it meant beating to windward instead of making a broader reach on an alternative course.

Every inch of the way the wind freshened up and the night was inky black, although the visibility of lights was very good. By the time we had reached mid-channel at the NF4 and NF5 buoys we had all the sea we wanted and, as the wind had veered to the west we were not running before it. The seas at this spot were confused - mostly under our stern - but from time to time one larger sea would come at us from nearly abeam to starboard, and we took quite a bit of water aboard over the starboard side.

The guests had retired below hours earlier where they had succumbed to seasickness and it was about here that Phil's stomach decided that it was not designed for this kind of thing. He disappeared below, too, leaving only Allan to help me.

Allan Wright is a born seaman; the worse it became, the better it appeared to suit him and I could not have had a better hand to help me under the circumstances. He has since gone regularly as a mate in coastal sailing barges and I can imagine him making a good one.

Topsy, carrying her full mainsail and jib, was travelling faster than I had ever known her run before but I found her to be almost uncontrollable and I had to fight the wheel to keep her on her course and to prevent her gybing.

An uncontrolled gybe occurs when the wind, instead of filling the sail hits the foreside which crashes the sail and boom suddenly to the opposite side. When this happens it can have fatal results, with broken spars and a yacht completely out of control. My greatest fear was that the boom might bring up hard against the starboard runner, the adjustable back-stay of the mast, and break itself - or worse. Just in case it did do so, I had Allan slack it away. It was as well that he did.

My arms ached and my back felt as though it was breaking. The light in the compass binnacle was too bright and seemed to mesmerise me and tired my eyes badly.

On the crest of one large wave from astern it happened. I was just too late to correct the yawing and for a second the boom lifted and poised. Then, with a thunderous crash, the mainsail gybed over. It was a horrifying moment when I expected the worst to happen - to feel something part and to see a tangle of wreckage where my spars were so beautifully set up just a moment before. But, by a miracle, nothing did part or carry away.

It was the worst gybe I have ever experienced. The boom came over from port to starboard more quickly than I could say 'knife' and it caused the yacht to turn rapidly to port until she was beam on the next sea, which poured aboard over the port rails. After taking one more sea abeam, I was able to steady the yacht back to a course where the wind was on the port quarter.

Obviously we had to gybe again to get back onto our course, but certainly not with the kind of gybe we had just experienced. By shortening the mainsheet and steadying the yacht at the precise moment of gybing, it was accomplished reasonably gently. The yacht was being overdriven and only by shortening the sail and reducing speed through the water could I correct her tendency to yaw about. Tired as I was, and with only Allan to help me, I had to find an easier and quicker way of shortening sail than by bringing the yacht head to wind and reefing in the approved manner.

Oh, the folly of carrying too big a spread of canvas and running for too long. I wonder how many fine sailing boats have come to disaster because of that very fault on the part of their masters.

The desired effect was achieved by lowering the gaff until it was almost horizontal, and *Topsy* became at once tractable, although the ballooning sail did itself some damage as it chafed on the port shrouds. To this day, the sight of the repairs in the mainsail reminds me of the run that night.

To prevent another episode like that happening in the future, I have fitted the loose footed mainsail with a tack tackle and I can now trice the luff of the sail upon the mast in the fashion of fishermen. I have never had cause to regret the adoption of this type of temporary reefing which has stood me in good stead several times since.

On board Topsy in heavy seas

Young Allan left the deck often to have a look around below and he would return to give a cheery but lurid description of the chaos in the cabins and the ghastly appearance of everyone below decks. He thought it was a huge joke to be able to tell me how he had found Mr B hanging head and shoulders out of his bunk, in no state to help himself back into it, and how Phil was groaning aloud as though on his death bed. How strange it is that those who seem to be immune to *mal-de-mer* can see something very comical in watching others suffer.

One thing has always puzzled me. Why is it that I always seem to speak to the only people on a trip to the Channel Islands who were not seasick during the run? I have met many who say that out of 200 people aboard only they and their wives and sometimes - they will very modestly admit - two other couples had to breakfast alone. What happens to the other 194 passengers? I see nothing shameful in admitting to suffering from seasickness and if you cannot help it, there is certainly nothing to do about it.

The first trawler I served in during the war made me seasick several times. She was a little flush-decked Aberdeen vessel called HMS *Onetos* and her motion could be horrible. Only those in the crew who had been professional trawler hands seemed to be able to stand it.

After I had left her, I was once following her into Dover harbour in HMS *Ronso* when I saw her almost capsize. We were returning from a 'shoot', more properly known as towed target gunnery practice off Folkestone. The shoot had been abandoned as the weather changed suddenly and it blew up until the sea became too mighty for the target towing vessel. On the way back HMS *Onetos* was in front of HMS *Ronso,* as she was the last ship of the first group of ships and HMS *Ronso* was the leading ship of the second group. As HMS *Onetos* turned ahead of me to enter the eastern dock, bringing herself abeam to the seas, she keeled over to port into a sea that she took aboard her throughout her entire length. Then she rolled right over to starboard until I saw her port bilge keel come out the water for a second or two.

She lay on her starboard side pinned down by the weight of water aboard her rushing down to her leeward side. Chief Skipper Tucker RNR could do no more than ring down 'Stop' to the engine room and I could see his white face peering at me as he pulled himself upright by gripping the dodger rails. I brought HMS *Ronso* up close the leeward side of the ship in order to pick up any of the crew who might be lucky enough to escape should she go the rest of the way. HMS *Onetos* hung like as was for what seemed to me to be an age. To her crew, especially those in the engine room, it must have seemed like eternity. The she recovered her upright position in a series of violent jerks.

The commander of minesweepers, or CMS, received a report from the skipper and he asked me my opinion of the vessel as I had once served in her. I told him that I was convinced that one night she would proceed to sea and never come back, so he put her off operations to have a stability test. The test report read: "Highly dangerous, unfit for sea".

All this was brought about by the never-ending additions to her armament and armour plating which had taken place at each refit. Thirteen tons of top weight had to be removed and 20 tons of ballast added before she was pronounced as seaworthy. In my opinion, it was not a surprise that any of us in her were seasick, but an absolute miracle that any of the crew were not!

I have gone off my course, so I shall get back to it again and continue on our trip to Holland.

From NF9 buoy, which marks the junction of the swept channels leading into Ostend, the motion of the yacht was by no means so severe and once more the gaff was hauled right up and the mainsail set correctly.

Upon hearing me tell Allan that I could see the twin spires of Ostend Cathedral, a very seedy looking Mr B made his appearance on the deck.

To sail into a strange harbour with a short crew would have been asking for trouble, so I decided to lower the sails out in the Ostend Roads and then motor in. There was a considerable swell in the roads and, although it was not particularly felt while Topsy was under her mainsail, the rolling became very pronounced when the sail no longer controlled the boat.

Our troubles were still not over. Phil nearly passed out when the boom hit him in the chest and pushed him with his back hard up against the dinghy. I saw his face blanch as he dropped down. I fully expected that he had broken a rib or two but, happily, he had only had the wind knocked out of him and suffered a few nasty bruises.

The reason we were unable to completely control the swinging of the boom was because the mainsheet block travelled across a horse that spans the cabin top. Since then I have had metal clamps made to hold the mainsheet block in the centre of the horse and, with only a maximum of about a foot float on the boom after it has been sheeted hard home, we have had no more injuries caused by it.

HMS Onetos - the never ending additions to her armaments made her a rolling hell

It was as well that we motored into the harbour because we found that just inside, on the starboard side, it was half blocked by the wreckage of a crane that had been tipped over the quay.

This was the first of many surprises in post-war continental harbours where wartime damage was still clear to see. Harbours, locks and jetties were damaged and the wrecks of shipping littered the coastal routes. We saw another side to the aftermath of war in the ports of Holland, France and Belgium which made the continuing problems of rationing and shortages at home seem tolerable by comparison.

We anchored near what used to be the yacht club and immediately set about launching the dinghy as one lady aboard, who was a Catholic, wanted to attend mass. Although they had been ill for the majority of the run, the passengers recovered in remarkably quick time as soon as we were in harbour. After rowing them ashore, Allan and I turned in for a spot of very welcome sleep.

Later in the day, we made friends with an English speaking Belgian named Charley Holbrook who brought his 12 year old son Constantine with him. If there was anything that we were unable to obtain, Constantine would get it for the reward of an English cigarette. We found him most useful.

Ostend was a very disappointing town for me and after the guests had spent one day visiting Bruges, we pushed on past Blenkinburg, Zeebrugge and Breskens into the West Schelde, where we moored up at Terneuzen in Zeeland.

The Belgium coastal routes ran through veritable graveyards of big ship wrecks - many of them unmarked by buoys. More wrecks lay in the entrance to Zeebrugge and Flushing harbour was almost closed by them. As we sailed past Flushing, we could see the evidence of the hammering that the town and port had taken during the war and when we arrived at Terneuzen we were surprised to find that it was in good shape, except for the lock gates and one dock in the centre which was in a sad state due to war damage. The place looked very much as it had done for years - and it is a delightful little place.

All the buildings and houses are invariably clean and painted up in gay colours. Cleanliness to the Dutchman is second nature and nowhere could one find boats kept in a more spotless condition than are their river barges.

I was amused when I saw a milkman's horse automatically stop after he had fouled the road with droppings. The old horse was so used to being pulled up so that the driver could sweep up the mess with a hand broom, shovel and bucket, which are invariably carried at the rear of each cart, that it had become second nature for the horse to stop each time and he required no pulling on the reins.

The Dutch people were very despondent over their prospects for the future. They told me of villages flooded, polders under water and bridges destroyed. Altogether they were not very hopeful of post-war recovery.

At the Cafe de Schelde, we sampled Dutch beer which we voted as being not too bad, but nowhere near the standard of English beer.

Two days later we sailed and motored up the Ghent canal to have a look at that ancient Belgium city. It was so quiet along one section of the canal that aboard the yacht we could hear the cows tearing up the grass along the tops of the banks. At the border town of Sas-van-Ghent we had to go through both the Dutch and Belgium customs within half a mile of each other.

Ghent is a city of wonderful architecture, untouched by the war, and I spent an interesting afternoon simply strolling around and looking at the grand buildings. Unlike Holland, we found everything we could possibly want was plentiful in the shops in Ghent, although the prices were high. At least, we thought that they were expensive at the time but I have lived to see such prices in our own country accepted as being quite in order.

We did not find the 100 per cent hospitality in Belgium that we had experienced in Zeeland. Holland stands united behind their Queen in no uncertain manner but Belgium is a divided country. I found two English speaking Belgians who openly admitted that they had preferred German rule to British and American liberation. There was a special bitterness against the Canadians who, they said, fought and smashed the town up after a few drinks of cognac, whereas the German soldiers were perfectly disciplined and caused very little trouble. Still you meet all types of people with all kinds of different convictions and I have met many Belgians whose opinions were just the reverse.

Like all the Dutch canals and rivers, the Ghent canal is really most uninteresting and after two days in the city we returned to Terneuzen. While we were waiting for the lock to operate we were besieged by gipsy children demanding cigarettes in very American English. After doling out a few to them we became tired of giving extra ones for their probably non-existent brothers and told them that we had no more to spare. Although the oldest child could not have been more than 14 years old and the youngest one was about four, we were treated to the finest example of 'Billingsgate' I had heard for a very long time when we refused to give any more cigarettes away.

At the Cafe de Schelde with the owner, Monsieur Cattoir

Back in Terneuzen we revisited our friends, the Cattoirs, at the Cafe de Schelde and on the last night we were in town we had a very fine time. After the cafe closed at midnight, Mama asked us down below to their private quarters and then entertained us with Dutch folk songs and very good Dutch drink.

We left Terneuzen at high water and carried the ebb against a very fresh south west wind. Off Flushing we found the sea more than we wanted. The fresh south westerly wind against the strong ebb kicked up a sea that was short, steep and appeared to be curling. *Topsy* was very wet, indeed. The motion, through being rapid, was most uncomfortable, so we decided to take shelter in Flushing harbour.

Overleaf: Flushing suffered massive devastation from bombing, German action and the flooding that followed

To enter Flushing we were forced to sail almost ashore on the starboard side, in order to round the wrecks in the harbour mouth, and inside we could see no possible berth because of the terrible devastation. Fortunately,

we were able to moor the yacht across the stern of four British minesweepers and to enjoy the comfort of a bath and drink aboard one of them.

We found Flushing to be in a pitiable condition. The railway station was in ruins, broken war equipment and rubbish was strewn everywhere, and to the right of the road leading into the town the countryside was underwater. It was very depressing. One small section of the town had escaped damage but the rest was a shambles with the majority of the residents living in pre-fabs, Nissen huts and wooden structures. On leaving Flushing next day we once more found ourselves punching head winds and seas with the passengers not feeling too well.

Knowing that we could not make way against the next head tide, I put into Zeebrugge where we took the mud alongside the Mole made famous by the epic raid in the 1914 war. The harbour was silted up very badly and dredgers were working hard to clear a way through to the locks of the Bruges canal.

The passengers went ashore and when they returned they told me that they would rejoin the yacht at Ostend as they had been told ashore that there were still mines sunk in the mud in Zeebrugge harbour. One fishing boat and a dredger had been casualties within the last week. So the crew and I took *Topsy* round to Ostend on the next high water while the passengers went by train.

On the morning we left Ostend we had some fun with another English yacht. In the NF Channel when we were near to each other, the owner of the other yacht asked us if we would like some Dutch gin and offered to pass a bottle to us. This was much easier said than done as both yachts were under full sail, and whereas we were gaff rigged and therefore sailing off the wind, the other yacht was Bermudan and could sail closer to the wind than we could. After a lot of jigging about we were able to sail close enough to each other for the owner to attempt passing the bottle with the aid of a fishing rod and line. But at the very moment that the bottle came within reach, it slipped out of the noose and disappeared. It was a bitter disappointment to our dry ship.

The Channel could never have been calmer than it was that day and we made no way through the water at all until sunset when a fine fresh breeze from the north gave us a six knot average run from NF5 to Dover.

NEVER A DULL MOMENT

Holland again after a fast and rough run to Terneuzen before a fresh south west wind. My two crew on this run were Reg Markham and a new hand, Jack Brigginshaw, who had been an engineer in the merchant service. Jack is one of those people with a rare sense of Cockney humour and he was an amusing hand to have along with us.

In Holland we experienced the same hospitality as we had on the last run, but after one day at Terneuzen we pushed on up the West Schelde to Antwerp.

At Antwerp we could find nowhere to berth until we saw an official waving us into the locks leading to the South Docks. We almost entered before the bridge had swung as the throttle of the engine went haywire just as we put our bows in. We were astonished when a brass bound official nearly fell on our necks and welcomed us saying: "We were expecting you yesterday but we have kept your berth vacant in the north east corner alongside the yacht *Cap*."

How they knew we were coming to Antwerp I could not tell as we had only decided ourselves the day before. We were to learn better later.

As soon as we had tied up, the passengers pushed off to see the shops while the crew and I wandered along the quay in search of a cafe. We found one that was nice and quiet, and settled down to a drink. The proprietress apparently thought that we might be musical. She was quite right. We were very musical, which is the reason why we left the cafe in such a great hurry when she started up a ghastly bellowing monstrosity of a mechanical organ, complete with drums and cymbals, which had bellows squashing in and out, rods shooting up and down and all other kinds of paraphernalia with brass knobs on. The din was appalling and could be heard across the other side of the dock. Any conversation was impossible, so we 'let go fore and aft' and got under way again, returning to the yacht where we found trouble, in the forms of the dock master and his assistant, awaiting us.

There appeared to be a war on between somebody and somebody else. As all the conversation was in Flemish, I did not have a clue what it was all about but I guessed that we were included in it somewhere. We were. According to the English speaking assistant he had been severely taken to task by the DM for welcoming us and giving us a berth as the name of the yacht was wrong. It should have been *Colin Archer,* not *Topsy.*

"You'll have to go out again," said he.

"It can't be done," I answered.

"Why not?" said he.

"Because we've broken the return spring on the throttle control and can't run the engine without a new one. If we must go out, you will have to tow us," said I.

"We have not got a launch here," said he.

I shrugged my shoulders.

There followed an interlude of ten minutes filled up in no uncertain manner by a Flemish duet between the DM and ADM. At last they reached a decision. We must move *Topsy* three feet further away from the quay. We did so and the two officials left, both very pleased with themselves as they had moved us.

The curtain came down on the final act when *Colin Archer* arrived next day and tied up alongside us with no trouble at all. I had expected something around the 80 ton mark by the fuss the dock master had made but I found that *Colin Archer* was really a fine little yacht around 12 tons.

With an hour of good drinking time wasted, we three again went in search of a cafe and settled on one kept by Franz Bels who had spent most of his life serving in British merchant ships. We found ourselves very welcome there.

Next morning it was blowing very hard from the south west. It made no difference to *Topsy's* lack of motion in the dock, but it did drive all the filth and even dead dogs up into the north east corner which is especially reserved for yachts.

The passengers had been ashore all the forenoon and returned to change into their best clothes to visit a friend in Brussels. During the time that they were aboard the lock gates were left open for a while in a falling tide so that the plank from *Topsy* to the quay was somewhat steeper than when they returned to the boat. One lady, upon walking ashore across the plank informed her husband, who was following her that the "plank was awfully near the edge, darling."

Before anything could be done about it he had progressed half way up the plank when the inevitable happened. In the twinkling of an eye he was transformed from a resplendent gentleman complete with Guards tie, into a filthy oil-stained swimmer doing the breast stroke amongst the dead dogs.

The effect upon the Belgians along the quayside was extraordinary. Everybody shouted at everybody else. They tore around in short circles in a state of great excitement, jumping onto boats and off again, while the gent's wife sat on the dockside bollard surveying the scene and, like little Audrey, she laughed and laughed and laughed.

Although the whole act began with the poor gent falling into the water it did not seem to occur to anyone to end it by pulling him out. When it was eventually done, the poor fellow was a very sorry looking spectacle and he did not smell any too good either, so the trip to Brussels was stood down until later.

The elderly gentleman who owned *Cap* stood chatting to me next morning. His English was absolutely perfect and he informed me that he had been educated at Walton-on-Thames. But he amazed me when he said: "I am very vexed this morning. I went up to the

Antwerp with Topsy taking pride of place next to the white yacht, Cap

city and purchased such a nice anchor for *Cap* but when I reached the quayside I dropped it and broke it in half. It was careless of me."

For a moment I wondered whether he was all there or whether we were having some sort of basic language misunderstanding. Anchors do not break in half when they are dropped.

Nevertheless, I commiserated with him and asked to see this wonderful anchor that could be broken by simply dropping it on the ground. In all seriousness he went forward along *Cap's* deck and actually returned with an anchor broken in two pieces. It certainly was a lovely looking stockless anchor, beautifully enamalled in black, but the shank was broken in half and I found on inspection that it was made of a very inferior cast iron. It was the first and only anchor I have seen that could be broken by being dropped. Maybe these Belgian yacht anchors are perfectly alright in the soft muddy bottoms of Dutch rivers, but what happens when they hit a hard bed?

When we left England, Reg, Jack and I were signed on as crew to *Topsy* which meant we could travel without passports as we would be returning to the country on the same British registered yacht. Less conveniently, it also meant we were only able to take £5 away with us and by the end of the week in Antwerp we were all stony broke. But a solution to this problem came along in a most unexpected manner.

Finding that I had a packet or two of Woodbines to spare, Jack and I went to the cafe and sold one packet to Franz for 20 francs. With beer at five francs a glass, we could at least buy a few drinks. When we entered the cafe we found it was empty except for a tall, well built and smartly dressed Belgian sitting with a woman at a table in the corner. I noticed that he and the woman drank only the most expensive drinks and that he was in a very jovial mood. In short he was getting 'very nicely, thank you.'

Franz told us that he was a rich merchant in the city who only came into the cafe once a fortnight when he went out on a real bender. For the rest of the time he did not drink at all. During the evening, the cost of his drinks was put down on a sheet of paper and I was amazed at the amount it totalled, but Franz told me that there were times when the gentleman spent £30 per night if his friends were in the cafe.

Jack and I with just a few francs to our name, were sitting on high stools at the bar chatting to Franz and his wife when a Scottish engineer came in. He was pretty well tanked up but was in no way troublesome as he simply bought a beer and sat down at the same table as the Belgian. Under his arm he carried a neat brown paper parcel.

Hearing English spoken, all be it very Clydeside, I asked him which ship he was from and he answered that he was from a British ship lying in the docks and bound for China in the morning. We were ready for anything from this red-headed Glaswegian, but he chatted amiably and told us that the parcel contained his lunch, packed for him by 'his boys'.

He opened the parcel to see what he had to eat and then, with a long face, pushed it along the table away from him. The 'boys' had certainly packed it up for him. I have never seen a more useless collection of eatables in my life. The parcel contained two raw potatoes, a stick of rhubarb, one onion, half a loaf of stale bread and a large blob of butter.

The big Belgian surveyed this assortment of food in a comical kind of way, picking up each object and pretending to inspect it, using his drinking glass as a magnifying glass. Then with a wry face and a sad shake of his head, he placed each sorry specimen back in the parcel. Then he pretended to discover the butter and, taking a small penknife from his pocket, he sampled it making exaggerated noises of enjoyment.

The Scotsman sat on his seat holding his glass of beer looking for all the world as if he was falling asleep and then suddenly, without a word, he went red in the face with temper and threw his glass at the bar where it smashed to tiny atoms, splashing its contents over Jack and me.

The effect was electric. The big Belgian, with his eyes staring and veins standing out on his brow, roared like a bull and, with one hand, flung the table away from him. In a second all was pandemonium with chairs and tables toppling about in all directions and Franz hanging onto the Belgian like a

Facing page: Ready to go ashore. Arthur Emmett with guest Harold Mosely

terrier. Jack went to his assistance while I closed with the Scotsman.

"He canna eat my butter," he screamed.

"Shut up Jock," said I. "Get to hell out of here before you're picked up. You didn't want it anyway. If they put you in the clink and you miss your ship, where the hell will you be then. Don't be a BF."

"But I want a drink," said Jock, a little cooler already.

"Go and have one somewhere else. There's a cafe every few yards," I reasoned with him.

While this was going on, we were weaving all over the place completing the general scene of destruction. I was holding onto Jock and getting into his way to prevent him reaching the Belgian. Jack and Franz were doing the same with the Belgian on the other side of the cafe. Jack left the Belgian to Franz and came over to help me, and together we literally talked the Scotsman out into the street to get rid of him.

As we were going back into the cafe there was a roar from inside. The Belgian came careering towards me in the doorway with a carving knife in his hand. Franz was picking himself up from the floor behind. The big Belgian had overcome Franz and taken the knife from behind the bar, presumably to go after the Scotsman.

Jack and I could see we were no match for him - even without the knife - for Franz was a stronger man than the pair of us put together and he had been defeated. I thought that we were for it, especially as we had no time to get out of his way.

In desperation I shouted at him: "Put down the knife" and pointed at it. To my utter amazement the Belgian stopped short, looking at the knife in his hand in a daze, for all the world as if he had only then realised that he had picked it up. Without a word he laid the knife on the only table that was still upright in the whole cafe and went back to his corner as meek as a lamb.

Wondering what would happen next, Jack and I returned to our stools at the bar and silently continued to down our drinks. Reflected in the mirror at the back of the bar, I could see the form of the big Belgian approaching us and Jack and I were ready for anything. But when he came up to us he put his huge hands on our shoulders and called us in French "mes bons camarades." He told Franz to give us a drink.

Later, he paid his account, plus extra to cover the damage, and went off in a taxi as Jack and I breathed huge sighs of relief. Franz pushed two beers across the bar to us, but when I went to pay for them with my last ten francs, he told me that they were already paid for by the Belgian who had deposited enough money behind the bar to last us in drinks all night. Then he handed me 1,000 francs which, he said, the Belgian had left with instructions that we were to take it. You could have knocked me down with a feather. It is the only time I have left a bar with more money than I had on me when I went in.

Next morning we left Antwerp and sailed to Terneuzen, where we stopped for one day. We left Terneuzen with the usual south west wind against us and our progress, tacking in fairly heavy seas, was very slow. The engine was of little use as the magneto had developed a fault causing the motor to run well for a while and then to fire intermittently.

By nightfall, after twelve hours sailing, we had only reached NF9 buoy. It was obvious that the weather was getting worse and from time to time we were lashed by bad rain squalls. At NF4 buoy we met particularly heavy seas and extremely strong gusts of wind hit us. I heard something go with a crack like a pistol shot and, at intervals, I heard the same sound repeated but in the darkness I could not see what it was.

Very soon I noticed that the mainsail was no longer set up as it should have been, but that it was ballooning out. All the lashings along the gaff and down the mast hoops had parted and the only thing to do was to lower the mainsail in order to save it. At that time I did not carry a tri-sail aboard and the only course for us was to put about and run under head sails only. While we were fighting to lower the mainsail and to get it under control, a dark shape loomed up right in front of our our starboard side only a hair's breadth away. The yacht had no lights and the owner was obviously single-handed, unable to do anything more than run before the wind

On board *Topsy,* the crew double-lashed the mainsail to the gaff once more, so that we were able, with one reef in, to reset it for our run into Ostend.

At dawn we saw the yacht that had narrowly missed hitting us the night before, about one mile ahead of us and still running before the gale. He undoubtedly would have been alright as his course would take him along the Belgian coast and right into the West Schelde river. We passed NF9 again at 6.50am and at 10am we entered Ostend under the engine which decided to behave itself for a short while.

Dawn and a calm sea

At Ostend we found ourselves out of bread and we had no permits to obtain any in Belgium, but I contacted Charley Holbrook and he came to the rescue. How he could obtain bread for us without permits I could not see, but after a lengthy conversation with the girl behind the counter in the baker's shop he told us that we could have five loaves.

"Will you please thank the young lady?" said Charley "She has given you her permits."

This we did, very naturally, but I was still mystified. Outside the shop I asked Charley how he had managed it.

"Oh," he said, "I just told here that you had been shipwrecked, had an awful time, and that all you food had been spoiled by salt water."

The rotten old liar - but he did the trick.

The weather moderated during the day and in the next forenoon we left Ostend in a fairly light wind, but it did not last long because by NF7 buoy the wind again freshened, giving us a heavy swell again at NF4.

Arriving in the Thames Estuary we received a south west gale warning for that area over the radio, so we decided not to carry on to Maldon but anchored in the lee of Margate, twelve hours from Ostend.

RUNNING-AND STALLING

T hat autumn I found a new job delivering or 'running' ships for other people. I found it very interesting and lucrative as I was not wearing out the gear on my own yacht. I had never expected to tread the bridge of a minesweeper of any description again, but within a year of leaving the Navy I found myself doing that very thing.

A local firm, May and Butcher, was purchasing a number of ex-Royal Navy minesweepers which were lying at various points around the coast. They had to be brought to Heybridge where they would be overhauled and refitted for resale.

The company had engaged a skipper, who was a deep-water man hailing from the west coast, to carry out this work. Like many west coast men, he had an unholy fear of the sands and shallow water of the Thames estuary and of the east coast in general but he was quite at home down south and west. On one run he took the ship around the deep water route via the Kentish Knock and Sunk - a long way round to reach Heybridge - and on another run he engaged a Trinity House pilot to guide him all the way from Dungeness into Heybridge.

This sort of thing made the runs a slow and costly business to May and Butcher, so they contacted me and asked if I would go with the skipper to act as navigator and pilot for a run from Salcombe in Devon. Having little to do with the yacht at that time, I very gladly accepted the offer.

I travelled to Salcombe by train and made my number with the skipper who I found to be a very likeable fellow. We got along together very well. He was about my age, of tall and slender build and looking smart wearing his ex-Royal Navy battledress. During the war he was in command of a deep sea tug and he told me many colourful stories of towing and of salvage at sea.

The ship we were to bring back was in a deplorable condition although, as I found out afterwards, she was probably one in a better state of preservation. In the Service these motor minesweepers were kept in a spotless condition and carried a crew of 22 or 24, but this Mickey Mouse outfit boasted just eight crew and three of these were one hundred percent landsmen who worked for the firm.

The ship was filthy through lying idle so long and she smelt damp, cold and stale. There was very little comfort aboard her, although I was better off than the others as I was given the 1st lieutenant's small cabin. Down below rats scampered about.

When I think of the chances we took in those old Naval throw-outs, I am surprised that we worked them around the coast without a loss. I never brought one around that had an accurate compass because they had already been stripped of all their sweeping gear and gadgets in the wheelhouse and on the bridge and the compass corrector coils were very often out of gear. Coupled with the fact that we carried the same two compasses from ship to ship and used them without 'swinging' ship, it is a wonder that we did not end up in China. Whenever it was possible to do so, I checked my compasses because I found that the deviation when known did not always stay constant.

Very often these old minesweepers were in a leaky condition and only the efficiency of the pumps kept them above water, but thanks to Johnny Boulter, the chief engineer, they always functioned and the main engine always got us home.

Johnny was a Frenchman who served in the Navy throughout the war and afterwards married and settled in Plymouth. He would live alone aboard these hulks for weeks on end, working on the engines and taking pieces from one engine to transform another, so that one ship would become a runner able to tow the non-runner home.

The main engine of these sweepers were either made by Crossley or, in the cases of the Canadian-built minesweepers, by Fairbanks Morse. I found that the Canadian built ones were finished in a superior way to those of English manufacture and my old favourite was MMS 249, Canadian built and comfortable but by no means the fastest craft around. I had more trust in her, though, than many others although the fact that my trust was a little misplaced was brought home to me when I sailed in her to Norway a year later.

We steamed out of Salcombe and made Chichester Harbour with one main engine breakdown which delayed us for an hour in West Bay as we were approaching Portland Bill. At Itchenor we collected a non-runner.

We shackled the tow wire onto her, ready for sea-towing, and then proceeded down river with the tow alongside us.

I have no great liking for towing motor minesweepers alongside one another because these vessels are constructed with a deep end and wide rubbing strakes or wooden fenders along their sides which means that when two craft are run alongside each other, the fenders or rubbing strakes foul each time the vessels roll.

The skipper seemed to think that everything would be alright as we had plenty of old lorry tyres as fenders between the two vessels, but as we made our way out we ran abeam to the swell and the two ships rolled away from and into each other with such violence that the wings of their bridges collided, causing a great deal of damage. The towed vessel lost several feet of her rubbing strake. Except for this incident, our trip to Heybridge was trouble-free, although our speed had to be cut down from time to time when we encountered fog.

During the winter I was very lucky to obtain a twin cylinder Lister diesel engine which was fitted in the place of the nearly useless Navigator and once more we were able to steam at over six knots, while the saving in the cost of fuel made a very great difference to the earnings of the yacht. I thought that a lot of my troubles were ended with its installation - as indeed they were eventually - but in the beginning I had teething troubles with it and it let me down badly in May 1948 on an attempted crossing to France.

One of the Naval throw outs - MMS 249, a Canadian built minesweeper

As a financial setback with an unparalleled number of mishaps, this journey takes the biscuit and I hope such a series of misadventures will never be repeated.

After a very severe spring, the weather did not appear to be able to make up its mind about what it wished to do and we were subjected to several periods of freakish weather which I had experienced before.

Usually one associates thunderstorms and lightning with very hot weather, but I have seen this type of weather when it was quite cold. Many a time I have met people who believe that whenever there is fog there will also be a flat calm with no wind. This is so most of the time, but I once experienced a gale of wind and a fog at the same time in the Dover Strait. I know of nothing worse. Normally in a fog one can ring down 'Stop' on the engine telegraph when you want to listen to pick up the bearing of a bell buoy or a light vessel's siren, or to approximately fix the position of another vessel whose siren has sounded near to you. But when fog combines with a high wind and a rough sea, this is not possible because you must steam to hold your course and the rule of 'Ease her, Stop her, Go astern' does not apply. A very jumpy thing is a gale of wind when you cannot see where you are going.

It was during such a period of freakish weather as this that Eric Albert approached me with the idea that he and some friends from Hornchurch should take a trip over to France. Tall bespectacled Eric kept the Thatcher's Arms at Warley and at that time he was also running the *Viking Saga*, then the largest passenger boat on the River Blackwater, from the promenade at Maldon. He wanted to have a holiday while he was able, for his working season was approaching and he would have very little chance later on.

With Eric and another friend of mine, Derek Roberts, as crew and with four other men aboard, we left Maldon under the diesel engine against a fresh east wind. We made fairly good way to the Raysand Channel and had reached a position abreast of the Buxey beacon when the engine slowed down as though on to one cylinder and water began to squirt out of the normally dry exhaust pipe. The cylinder head gasket must have blown.

We went to anchor and later took the ground as the tide fell. We removed the cylinder head and found that the gasket had indeed blown and as we had no spare aboard, we made one out of Hallite. With this improvised gasket fitted the engine appeared to run properly once more.

As soon as we refloated we continued under the engine towards West Buxey buoy, but it was very soon apparent that there was something very wrong with the Lister which ran hotter and hotter. I found that the water pump was cold and working efficiently but the cylinder head was so hot that the paint was blistering. I was baffled and, after hoisting the mainsail, I stopped the engine.

With the flood tide the wind had changed to south west and so, on an easterly course through the Whittaker to the Barrow Light Vessel we made good way under sail only although, with the wind against the tide, we had a sharp, short and uncomfortable sea.

At the Barrow Light Vessel we were against the tide once more as the ebb started to run down the Barrow Deeps. We made very little way over the tide, tacking to windward. We attempted to restart the Lister to help us as far as No 10 Barrow buoy, but we found that the cylinder head had cracked and the engine was useless.

Eric was working up forward and as we went about he took a very nasty smack in the face from the jib sheet. He had to retire temporarily from work. A short while later, a ghastly apparition in the form of one very seasick passenger crawled up the aft companionway from down below and, in a pitifully weak voice, asked that I should take them back home.

My fellow crew, Eric and Derek, were furious. Eric said that since they had come aboard with the express idea of going to France, I should take them there, whether they liked it or not.

"A cross-channel steamer wouldn't take them back," said Eric.

I agreed with him up to a point, but argued that if a taxi driver heading for Waterloo Station was asked, half way, to go to Liverpool Street Station instead, he would not force his fare to go Waterloo Station if he did not want to. So, I contended, we had to take the 'erbs back.

This was easier said than done because there was insufficient water through the Swin Spitway and we had to dodge about for hours before there was enough water for us to run through the Wallet.

When a squall hit us near the NW Knoll, *Topsy*, on the reach, went like a dingbat and Derek, who is a natural born helmsman, was in his element at the wheel. We carried a fine fresh sailing breeze all the way in to just off Bradwell where the wind fell away so suddenly that the yacht shot into an upright position still carrying her way with the mainsail flapping. Then the wind flew into the north west and hit us with a tremendous force. For two or three minutes *Topsy* leaned to the blast and I was afraid something would carry away. I told Derek to hold her as close up to the wind as he could but not to 'luff' because if he let the canvas flap we would surely have lost it in such a squall. With the wind came hail of such severity that it was impossible to face it and a less stiff craft than *Topsy* would have been knocked flat by the blast of the squall.

As suddenly as it had struck us, the wind dropped again and we found ourselves touching the mud on the south side of the river. There was nothing for it but to anchor and wait for the flood tide to make enough water to give us sufficient room to sail off the lee shore. We stowed the sails and waited. When sufficient water had made under and around us, we hoisted the mainsail once more, weighed anchor and, with a very light north west wind, stood across to Tollesbury pier. We were very slow in coming around to the next

Topsy leaving the Truman's brewery quay at Fullbridge, Maldon, with a new crew of guests

Overleaf: The Welcome Sailor, beyond the wooden bridge at Fullbridge, was one of the pubs that had a tide licence, allowing it to open whenever the tide was up

tack because *Topsy* only just had steerage way with such a light wind.

In 1947 the American Liberty ship *Helena Modjeska* broke her back on that graveyard of American ships, the South Goodwin Sands. Later she was salvaged and the two separate halves were towed to the River Blackwater where they were moored to a buoy. The forward half from just in front of her bridge to her bow was tied onto the buoy and the aft part - around the wrong way - was tied alongside the forward part, but not made fast to the buoy itself. In this fashion the two halves did not lie square alongside each other but, instead, they formed a V with its opening facing the tide. This meant that the ship was never true to the tide, nor did it stay in one position as do the other old ships moored up in the river. It swung about as the tide swirled around in the opening to the V, moving to the extent of its play on the mooring buoy from one side to the other.

Before *Topsy* could strike ahead after her very slow come about, the wind died completely so that a match struck on deck would not have flickered. In the position that we were occupying at the time, it was obvious that the strong flood tide would carry us up to *Helena Modjeska* and, with all way through the water lost, there was no means of steering *Topsy* out of the danger.

I said to Eric, quite calmly: "Do you know, we are going to hit that thing unless we get a puff of wind."

"Shall we let go the anchor?" asked Eric.

"It would do no good," I answered. "It would take longer to flake the cable over our old windlass than it will take to reach *Helena Modjeska* and we may pick up the buoy mooring with the flakes and be in a hell of a mess".

We stood together helplessly watching *Topsy* approach *Helena Modjeska*. The best we could hope for was a glancing blow along her sides. This would have happened in the case of a normal ship at anchor but, as we reached the wreck, she swung around in the tide as usual and we ran bows first clean into the V between the two halves. Our 17 foot bowsprit took the full force of the impact, bending almost impossibly before it snapped off short. As it was so early in the season, I had not refitted my topmast and cross-trees for which I was thankful. We would certainly have lost them and perhaps the main mast, too.

There we were, wedged tightly between two halves of a floating wreck of a big ship and pinned in there by the tide.

"Hey!" said a voice.

We looked around and saw a face peering at us from over the bows of the ship towering above us. The face wore heavy whiskers and on its head was a dirty old cloth cap. Its mouth was puffing away at a blackened clay pipe. A hand appeared and took the pipe over for a second.

"Hey," said the face again. "You should have called tomorrow. We wouldn't have been here. They're towing us to Grays in the morning".

The shipkeeper's statement seemed so ridiculous that we had to laugh in spite of the circumstances.

"What can we do now, Arthur?" asked Eric.

"Nothing at all until slack water," I answered and, lying down on the cabin top, I promptly went off to sleep.

At the change of tide a motor launch towed us out, stern first, and then towed us up the river as far as Thirslet Creek, where we anchored to await the tide. On the next flood tide I sailed the yacht up under mainsail and foresail and we moored up in Maldon sometime in the early hours of the morning.

When I examined the engine, I found that we had failed to punch out one waterway in the new Hallite gasket which was the cause of the over-heating.

The cost of the repairs to the engine and yacht for that trip came to a loss of about £1 for every hour that we were away from Maldon.

HOLLAND AGAIN

With a new bowsprit fitted, *Topsy* looked no worse for her mishaps and the Lister engine with a new cylinder head performed very well. In the middle of the season I took six lads of around 25 years of age to Holland. They were all ex-servicemen and they were the type I like to take away with me, for they go for a good time and everything that happens - rough or smooth - is an adventure to them.

We had smooth sailing as far as No10 Barrow buoy but after we had set our course south for the Edinburgh Channels I noticed a line squall approaching us, so we handed the topsail and triced up the mainsail. The squall hit us hard and, because one of the lads had not belayed the jib sheets properly on their cleats, my large jib blew adrift. It gave two flaps with a sound like a cannon firing and then disappeared in pieces to leeward. It took less time for this to happen than it has taken me to write the line.

With her jib missing, the yacht tried her best to come head to wind, but this was overcome by furling the mizzen sail and she cracked on in fine style under foresail and reefed mainsail. The wind freshened steadily after the squall had passed and we debated whether to carry on across or not. We decided that, as the anchorage in the lee of Margate was our only haven and from North Foreland we would have a beam wind, we should carry on with the second jib in the place of the one we had lost. The seas became heavier as we continued on our easterly course from the Foreland but, under the press of the full mainsail once more, *Topsy* was sailing comfortably.

We arrived in Terneuzen but after two days decided to press on for Rotterdam, entering the South Beveland Canal at Hanswerd. Before en-

Facing page: moored at Maldon - Topsy and Torfinn

tering the lock, we housed our bowsprit and removed the bumpkin and thought we would be able to avoid any damage with these two awkward extremities removed.

I had already been told by another cross channel sailor that he was amazed by the behaviour of the Dutch and Belgians in the South Beveland Canal. No matter how well and considerately they handle their ships elsewhere, they always seem to go absolutely mad when they are here. I found that observation true on this occasion.

We entered the lock and tied up alongside a Dutch canal boat to await the entry of all the other ships. We had no sooner hooked on to this boat than we received an impact up the stern that broke us adrift and did my quarters some damage. We shot ahead and damaged the name board of a boat ahead of us, much to the annoyance of its Belgian skipper.

We had been hit up the stern by a lighter carrying large pieces of rock to be used for repairing dykes. It had been towed in by a tug which had entered at a fair pace towing a large motor barge and two heavily laden lighters. Once in, the tug had gone full astern into the bows of the barge in order to stop his way. They crashed one into the other like a train shunting and, bouncing off each other, they hit anything and everything in their path. For a while there was quite a fuss going on but eventually everybody settled down again, waiting for the lock gates ahead to open and exercising what appeared to be infinite patience.

Suddenly the skipper of the boat next to us jumped up, tore into his wheelhouse and started up his diesel engine. Everybody else did the same. They had seen the sluice gates beginning to move. In England a skipper would wait for the gates to be completely open before letting go, but not so in Hanswerd, for while the gates were only two-thirds open everybody steamed ahead like mad with us in the middle of them.

Nobody waited to take their turn to go through the narrow exit from the lock but, with their engines banging and racking, they forced each other out of the way in order to be first. Maybe their vessels are designed to stand up to his kind of treatment but the yacht was not and she grunted and groaned as she was squashed between two motor barges. To try to handle the yacht was impossible because the wash from their screws swung her all over the place.

We eventually got through and pulled out of the way of these mad blighters who went tearing past us as if they had only five minutes to live. We followed in a more leisurely manner and, because of our high mast, we were delayed at two bridges. But when we arrived at the locks at Welmindinger we found all the barges were still in the lock and all the skippers were chatting and once more waiting with infinite patience.

Again, the first movement of the sluice gates turned this scene into a mad house, but this time we were not smashed about as we were last in the lock and their wash only pushed us hard up against the wall.

If anyone should wish to see the difference between English and European manners, the South Beveland Canal would supply a perfect example. I have not been through there since as I prefer to go to take the longer sea route around Walcheren Island.

We spent that night in the little harbour of Stoofpolder lying alongside a very nice Dutch barge yacht owned by a Belgian gentleman. His daughter spoke English perfectly and she told us that there had once been a very nice little village ashore but that it had been ruined when the Germans flooded the country.

The open waters of the Oude Maas leading to Rotterdam

We asked her if it was worth our while to go ashore and she answered that the Kermesse was on and that there was a fair. I have never been a lover of fairgrounds but I did want to see how the Dutch behaved at a Kermesse, which is really a sort of carnival where the usually solid and law-abiding Dutch take a night off from restrictions, self-denial and inhibitions to let their hair down.

It was all very strange to us ashore. We looked and felt complete aliens to the atmosphere and as the place was no larger than an Essex village, like Little Totham, and was populated mostly by farm labourers, the Kermesse was a very simple affair.

The fair had half a dozen stalls selling shellfish and eels, and one roundabout whose music was loud and discordant as it had only one note in the bass that worked and that note was always out of tune. The simple-hearted villagers enjoyed themselves more on this old roundabout than the average person at Clacton would have done on the scenic railway.

There were two cafes open until 2am and in one the villagers danced to a mechanical organ. In the other, four Dutchmen performed on accordions, so we tried that one after our experiences of mechanical music so far. Dancing in cafes is not allowed in Holland except during Kermesse and as there were no dance halls in the village, this cafe was crowded.

In the crowd were two girls from Amsterdam who, because they danced very well, were very much sought after by the lads from the yacht. One of the men, Peter Mann, was very short with a typical Army officer's moustache. Active and alert, he dances energetically with a style all his own.

Peter asked one of the girls from Amsterdam, who was rather tall, for a dance. They went onto the floor first and took a few steps before they realised that the dance was not the rumba they had expected but a selection by the accordions that sounded something like a Spanish fandango. They did not stop but carried on improvising steps perfectly while the local men and girls in the hall stood on chairs to watch what they imagined was an exhibition dance. I laughed until I nearly cried at the sight of short Jack-in-the-box Peter and the tall willowy Dutch girl performing intricate steps that nobody could recognise, while the Dutch around the hall wildly applauded and called loudly for encores at the end. Peter told me afterwards that he did not have a clue as to what step he was going to take next but the girl played up to him so well that they danced as if the thing had been previously rehearsed many times.

One of the revellers was a peculiar old boy of about 1890 vintage who wore a peaked cap and looked very much as if he had seen a lot of water in his time, although I rather think that it was mostly the water used in brewing beer. Nevertheless, we christened him the Admiral. I do not think there was a single English-speaker in the cafe that evening and, although the old boy was no exception, he attached himself to us. He was so friendly that we bought him a drink.

Did I say a drink? I should have said a dozen drinks. The more he had, the more he wanted and the more he beamed at us. He reminded me of a spaniel dog looking at you with friendly eyes and wagging tail, hoping that as you had already given him several biscuits you might give him yet another one if he looked at you long enough. The Admiral said nothing at all but just kept near to us wherever we went and beamed. His beaming became a little lop-sided after a while but he appeared to be happier than ever.

Suddenly his face froze and the spaniel look turned to a hangdog expression as a woman wearing ordinary indoor clothes with sleeves rolled to her elbows, stepped in through the door of the cafe and strode rapidly up to the Admiral. She stood with her hands on her hips and proceeded to give him a large piece of her mind in rapid and shrill Dutch. For the next five minutes she must have derated the Admiral from commissioned rank down to Stoker 2, while the poor old boy made ineffectual gestures indicating excuses. But he could not get a word in edgeways.

Everyone around us was roaring with laughter and then the woman, after getting short of breath but not of temper, took the old boy by his ear and led him out of the cafe to even more amusement.

The next day we sailed on the flood tide up to Dordrecht, a place I am rather fond of. This is a nice clean town and one section of it is most picturesque. My passengers were very disappointed because they wanted to go to a dance, but they found that all dancing in Dordrecht was banned by the Burgermeister. After one night in Dordrecht we carried on through the Oude Maas to Rotterdam where we tied up alongside the floating boathouse of the yacht club.

The best part of the city of Rotterdam was destroyed by bombing. Those forty-five or so minutes in 1940 must have been hell on earth for the Dutch. You can only really appreciate the extent of the damage when you compare aerial photographs of the city before and after the raid. We stayed for a week in Rotterdam and the men visited the Hague and Amsterdam. Then we returned to our own shores via the Galloper Light Vessel and the Sunk.

Within four days of returning to Maldon, I was on my way back to Holland once again, taking the same route as the previous trip with the exclusion of the South Beveland Canal. That time, I carried an ex-Army colonel and his wife and family. He was one of the few officers who got out of the trap at Arnhem. I stayed aboard the yacht in Rotterdam while he went to Arnhem by rail to show his family where the battle had taken place. We were very fortunate to be in Rotterdam that week as we were able to join in the celebrations when Queen Wilhelmina handed the throne to Princess Juliana. How the Dutch love the Orange and the Tulip. The decorations and illuminations were something really worth seeing.

Topsy in Rotterdam

After dark thousands of people went to the park and the riverside to see the lights. The river was a picture with a dredger and a tug, both illuminated all over, moored in the centre. Every ship and yacht, including *Topsy*, was dressed for the great day and we rounded the evening off in the Parkside where they gave a first class cabaret.

My last trip abroad that year was in October when I took the yacht to France, but the journey was uneventful compared to some of the earlier ones with nothing greatly exciting or out of the way happening although the weather was anything but kind.

NIGHTMARE JOURNEY

J anuary, February and March are always dull for me as there are few customers who want to go to sea during these months - and I do not blame them. One night in the first week of March I was sitting reading in front of the fire, wishing that I could find an excuse for going away to sea once more, for a month at home is usually all I can stand without becoming restless or finding myself in a groove where I do the same things at the same time every day of the week.

I had little hope that this boring routine would end before the summer season started, but somebody knocked on the door and I answered it to find Arthur Gurton from May and Butcher standing there. I immediately knew that this meant moving one of the old minesweepers somewhere. Arthur told me the firm had sent him round to see if I would take a minesweeper to Norway.

Would I go? I'll say I would. This was something different and - even better - the minesweeper was my old favourite, No 249.

That call came on a Thursday night and when I asked what day we were to sail, I was given the answer: "Monday to Harwich and Tuesday to Norway." This was very short notice as I would need a passport because I would have to leave the ship in Norway and fly home. All day Friday I was in London obtaining my passport while the shipping agent obtained passports for the crew and acquired the charts we would need.

I still have the clearance label for that trip. It reads: "Proceeding entirely at own risks". This was because the vessel was unregistered and therefore had no name, port of registry or nationality and could not fly the Red Ensign. Should we have to put into another country because of bad weather or because of trouble with the ship, we would not be under British protection in the event of the ship being seized. In marine law, these minesweepers were not ships, but hulks, unless they were registered.

To register 249 would have meant a great deal of trouble and expense and it was a very complicated business, so we had to take the risk. This state of affairs made me feel rather like a pirate - the Jolly Roger would have been an appropriate ensign.

Several minesweepers had been sold to foreign buyers but the Danes and Norwegians usually sent their own crews to collect them once they were registered as Danish or Norwegian vessels, but 249 was not wanted as a ship and had been purchased simply for her engine which was to be fitted in a new coasting ship being built in Kristiansand. To lift the engine out, crate it up and ship it to Norway would have been expensive, so it was decided to take it over under its own steam.

Harwich

On Monday we sailed to Harwich where we were busy immediately, storing up, bunkering and clearing Customs. On Tuesday morning we had a compass adjuster aboard and we swung the ship. But he seemed to find errors that I do not think existed as I had found little wrong with our course from the River Blackwater to Harwich. After giving me a deviation card showing errors of as much as six degrees, he departed expressing his dissatisfaction with the result of the swinging. This left me wondering who was correct. It was like having two watches - one that gained and one that lost - and not knowing which was keeping nearer to the correct time.

We were forced to take a Trinity House pilot out of Harwich to the Sunk and I told him nothing about the alleged six degree error on the compass, waiting instead for his reactions. He said nothing, so when we reached the Sunk I asked him how he had found the compass behaving on his courses. He answered: "Very well."

I decided to ignore the deviation card but to check on transits ashore wherever possible. While we were at sea I checked the compass by the bearing of the sun at sunset and sunrise and by the Pole Star and found little error.

We were a very small crew for such a trip and could not work proper watches. I was skipper, Bob Halls who was manager of the firm at that time, was mate and helmsman, Johnny Boulter was chief engineer and often helmsman as well. Second engineman Dennis Merry, Arthur Gurton and Mrs. Boulter, as cook, completed the crew.

We started with the engine running at 280 revolutions per minute which, with the tide, gave us a speed of 11.5 knots but, from the Smith's Knoll Light Vessel, Johnny eased the engine down to 260 revs which we maintained throughout the night, giving us a speed of 9.2 knots.

I noticed that on a light vessel in the position once occupied by the Swept Channel buoy, S2, a north gale cone was hoisted and the wind certainly was freshening from the north west.

No 249 was very light as she had been stripped down to her bare necessities. She began to roll in a not very satisfactory manner in the rising sea which she was taking on her port quarter and the helmsman - often me - had plenty of work to hold her on her course.

Johnny's wife had retired early the night before so that she could rise early to get us all a good breakfast, but the daylight found her in no state to do anything of the sort. Arthur Gurton went aft to the galley to get whatever he could, but a green sea curled over the quarter and washed out the galley fire, effectively putting paid to any hot meals or drinks for some time.

The Pit Light Vessel was not on station but we passed her marker buoy at 10.15am in a heavy sea with the engine revolutions reduced to 205. By 7.15pm we were, by dead reckoning, in the position which should have been occupied by the RH1 Light Vessel but its light was not visible so I concluded that it was not on station. There were many lights about which I took to be trawlers hove-to.

Our course altered here from approximately north east to north and so, from quartering the seas, we started to punch into them, taking them forward of the beam on the port side. The motion of the minesweeper became most uncomfortable.

I looked at the inclinometer on the binnacle and noted that we were rolling with a regular 25 degrees roll either way. It was impossible to stand on the bridge without holding onto something or wedging myself between the binnacle and the dodger.

Around midnight the seas became vicious and the wind was so strong I could only get my breath on the open bridge by turning my head sideways with my mouth wide open. I staggered down the companionway to the wheelhouse where Arthur was struggling manfully with the wheel. I found him in a very sorry state with his eyes streaming as he peered at the steering compass, being seasick where he stood. Through an opening in the floor the smell of hot oil and diesel wafted up making the whole wheelhouse a most unpleasant place.

The new second engineman showed great tact when he entered the wheelhouse and very quietly said to me: "Can I talk to you, Skipper?"

"Surely," I answered, "but why the secrecy?"

"I didn't want to say anything to anyone until I had spoken to you first. The Chief is off watch having a rest and I didn't like to call him unless it was absolutely necessary, but the main engine is moving," he said.

"Moving?" I asked. "What do you mean - shaking like they do with vibrations?"

"No, Skipper, it's moving up and down."

"UP AND DOWN?" I goggled at him.

"Yes, Skipper"

"Alright, I'll come down with you."

I left the wheelhouse to Arthur and went down to the engine room. If the wheelhouse was bad, it was horrible down there. Bilge water and oil ran from side to side with a nasty swooshing sound and the smell was positively sickening. Water which broke with great force whenever the vessel took a sea aboard - which was often - sounded far worse to me down in the engine room than it did on deck.

As I looked at the engine I saw its bed plates lift well over half an inch from the bearers as we rolled heavily to starboard and then fall back again with a clanking noise as we rolled once more to port, when the bed plate on the opposite side would lift. As far as I could see, only the exhaust pipes on the top of the engine and its own bottom weight were stopping it from rolling right over.

Should such a thing have happened, the very heavy engine would have gone broadside through the side and bottom of the vessel and we would have sunk like a stone without any chance of survival as our sea boat could not have been launched and neither would it have lived in such a sea. At best, if the engine did not go through the side, it would cause a heavy list, lying out of position, and we would have capsized or foundered anyway.

Bob Halls came down as we were examining the engine.

"What's the trouble, Arthur?" he asked.

I merely pointed to the engine as its bed plate left the bearer. Bob looked shocked.

"I'll be lucky if I see my wife and kids again," he said. We lurched over heavily and the engine lifted a little more than before.

"Call Johnny," I shouted and I struggled up the iron ladder as fast as I could. I fought my way back along the deck where twice I had to hold on while a sea which had crashed aboard swirled around us, but I made the wheelhouse safely and, taking the wheel from Arthur, I brought the vessel up to port, head to sea, and rang down 'Slow' on the telegraph.

Johnny came into the wheelhouse a short time later wearing only his shirt and trousers and dripping with water.

"There's nothing I can do, Skipper," he said. "The engine is fitted on wooden bearers and the threads of the holding down bolts - they've stripped. Can you put us in somewhere?"

"I've been thinking about it, Johnny," I answered. "There is only Ebjsburg -miles astern of us - and if I put about and run, there must be a time when we are turning that we will be right abeam to the sea and that's the time when that engine is going to roll out the side. We can only keep head to sea."

"But I don't like to keep the engine running," argued Johnny. "The propshaft - she may go next - there's so much strain on it. Can't we anchor?"

"We could do because we are in about 25 fathoms of water, but I doubt if we have cable enough aboard to be able to pay out sufficient to hold her in this sea and I know that these vessels roll even worse at anchor," I said.

Johnny knew that this was true as he had had enough experience of minesweepers and he went back to the engine room looking very glum. There was nothing that he or I could do to alter and improve the situation. We could only pray that nothing went wrong with the propshaft and that the pipes over the engine did not give way.

Hove-to with the engine at a minimum of 180 revs certainly improved matters, but even so it did not improve the rolling to a degree where we did not hold our breaths and listen for the fatal crash every time the vessel took a heavy lurch in one direction or the other.

With Arthur at the wheel again, I went on the bridge and was lucky to be able to take my latitude from the Pole Star while the visibility and the horizon were clear for a while. As I worked out the sight in the wheelhouse, I had to lean heavily against the chart table with my chest and stomach in order to stay in one place. Poor Arthur was still being sick and the diesel oil was still smelling horribly, but I felt alright. I went up to the bridge again to try to get another sight to confirm the one I had already obtained, and as I emerged through the trap door at the top of the companionway the ship took a heavy lurch to starboard. I was off balance and was thrown bodily across the bridge to bring up against the sides with a crash that knocked the breath from my body and ripped my sheepskin jerkin right across the back.

For a while I was dazed and shaken and then, as I struggled to get to my feet, I was very seasick for the first time in seven years since the days of the old *Onetos*. The long hours, no food or hot drink, the smell of diesel oil and sick in the wheelhouse, combined with the motion of the ship and the shaking up from my fall really gave me the works. For a while engines that moved and ships that rode out a gale did not interest me. Neither could I see the Pole Star.

This was at 3am and I had been on watch for a very long time, so after sticking it for a little longer, I handed over the charge of the ship to Bob, who was fresh and turned in, after noting that we were now past high water time and that the gale was abating and that our roll - thank God - was rarely reaching the point where the loose engine endangered us.

I took over again at 8.15am to find that the gale had blown itself out and that Bob had put the speed up to 260 revs. again. He had put the ship back on her course at 6am. The weather was not clear and it was not possible to see any horizon. The sun shone fitfully, but not clearly enough or long enough for me to get a sight, so we carried on by dead reckoning.

By midday we were steaming in dense fog which seems very prevalent along the Danish coast and in the Skaggerack, but we did not slow down as we had at least six hours more steaming to make a landfall.

My log for that trip for that evening reads: '1600 dense fog, stopped engine; 2005 dense fog, stopped engine; 2130 half speed ahead etc until we picked up the Ryvingen Light at 23.40.'

At 2.30 in the morning we stopped the engine off Kristiansand Fjord and signalled for a pilot. There was no wind or tide so we just lay where we were and the crew slept while I kept watch and saw the Norwegian dawn.

I had read of the beauties of the dawn in Norway but I had never expected it to be as beautiful as it was. My grandfather made many trips to Norway and in his house he had pictures showing the dawn in the fjords. They were unnaturally brightly coloured and I always thought that they could not possibly be true. They certainly were. For an hour I watched the sky show every shade of colour from black to emerald green, from brilliant blue to yellow and through gold and orange to red and, finally, normal daylight. As the rocks and mountains became visible, it was a truly wonderful sight.

The pilot came out at 0500 in a typical double-ended pilot cutter powered by a very slow running diesel engine that had an exhaust pipe like a six inch gun barrel and from which smoke rings puffed out into the still air. Wearing a Norwegian beaver style hat, he stepped aboard, shook hands and said: "Good morning, Captain, welcome to Norway."

When Bob spotted that hat he set his heart on possessing one and he did so as soon as we were ashore.

The impression I received as we steamed into the fjord was that the air was very sharp and cold and visibility was exceptionally good. You can see objects miles further away than in England and everything appears to stand out in the third dimension, probably because there is little dust in the air due to the rocky nature of the country, the water of the fjords and the forests of pinewood.

While we were steaming into the fjord, I worked my dead reckoning back to find that the ship only covered 18 miles in nine hours during the gale - an average of only two knots - while I had been allowing for four knots.

As time went by and we saw no shore lights, I had begun to wonder if the deviation card might have been correct after all on the course north, although I had not found that it was on the north easterly course as far as the position of the RHI Light Vessel. If the card was correct, then we would have been west of our course, and longitude and we would have been heading north along the Norwegian coast. But my faith in the compass was proved and our course to the Ryvingen Light had been correct. The only error was in allowing for more speed during the gale than the vessel actually did.

We tied 249 up alongside the new coaster that was to receive her engine, and the representatives of the Norwegian firm came aboard. When they had learned from the pilot that the engine ran very well coming into the fjord, they wanted us to take them out to see the way the vessel ran for themselves. Bob Halls put his foot right down and told them that as we had delivered the engine to them undamaged, he was not going to run it again. They could run it themselves after they had concluded the business of purchasing it.

"After the night before last, I won't go another inch in this ship, not even if you gave me a thousand pounds," he concluded.

We were disappointed ashore in one respect, for south Norway is dry. There are no public houses or cafes where one can sit and drink. A drink can only be obtained with a full meal at a hotel, so we did have a full dinner in the evening although it was nothing compared with the pleasure of having a drink in a cafe.

We thought south Norway was very strait-laced. It is a wonderful country for scenery and I would have liked to see more of it, but we elected to stay only two clear days and then return home.

We were very lucky to be able to watch the last ski-jumping competition of the winter season as the thaw had set in and snow was only visible on high ground or, as in the case of the ski-run, in the shelter of mountains and woods. The Norwegians turned out for the event in the same way that the English turn out for a football match and with as much enthusiasm. I was thoroughly interested in the whole affair but I could not for the life of me see why some of the competitors did not break their necks.

Even the spectators came close to danger. As the last competitor completed his run, everybody rushed home for tea and as they crossed a wooden bridge, en masse, their weight broke the bridge in half throwing a dozen or so of them into the stream below. By a miracle nobody was hurt and everybody laughed loudly. Even those in the water took it good temperedly and laughed as loudly as the rest.

We found that there was no airfield convenient to Kristiansand so we returned to Hull in the Wilson Line passenger/cargo vessel *Tinto*.

FRANCE WITH THE GUARDS

L ike the previous year, the summer of 1947 was nothing to write home about, being freakish, windy and wet for the majority of the time. Most of the yacht work was carried out around our coast and nothing outstanding happened until, at the end of the season, three Army officers approached me with a view to sailing to Spain. Being short of work at the time, I took the job on.

They were three very tall well-built gentlemen - a major and two captains in the 12th Royal Lancers - named Julian Fane, Paul Croxford and the Hon Anthony Lawther. I could not have wished for three finer shipmates on a yacht They had served very hard together in the Far East without home leave and their colonel had granted them six weeks leave at the same time. So they asked Harold Day, the harbour master at Brightlingsea, where they could charter a yacht with a skipper but no crew, and he sent them over to me.

Having made up their minds to go in *Topsy,* they worked out a schedule for the cruise. That is always a fatal thing to do. I have seen it attempted many times but always, perversely, these scheduled trips seem to attract more snags and trouble than any trip where the passengers take what comes when it arrives.

The first snag to the schedule was caused by the Government putting a ban on all foreign travel, except for commercial purposes, from October 5 and their colonel regretfully informed them that they would have to be back in England by October 4. With anyone other than these three gentlemen it would not have mattered as our return could always be delayed by bad weather, but to serving officers orders were orders when they came from the colonel - Government or no Government. This made Spain as a turning point completely out of the question, so the Channel Islands were declared as the destination.

We arranged that we would stand watches after we had passed Dungeness as none of them was familiar with the Thames estuary and Dover Strait. Julian was to stand a watch with me and Paul and Anthony took the other watch together. We did well until we were off the western entrance to Dover where the wind fell away altogether, leaving us rolling in a very heavy swell. Nothing in a yacht can be worse or more irritating than this. With all the gear aloft slamming from side to side and the sails slatting about, it was a most uncomfortable and annoying time.

I remember Mr Howells, who owned the ex-pilot cutter, *Olive*, telling me of an experience of heady swell that he had off the Lizard years ago. He made many long passages in this fine old sea boat, including one to Spain and another around the Baltic, but I do not know if he was in his own boat or another on this occasion. He told me that for over two days he was becalmed in a heavy swell within sight of the comfort of Falmouth harbour and the Helford river, but without an engine he could do nothing but drift up and down with the tide.

The noise of the gear up aloft slatting about and the motion of the vessel became so annoying that after hours of this sort of hell, everybody became on edge and irritable. Everything possible was tried to keep the yacht head onto the swell and to stop the movement of the gear but nothing was successful. In the end the sails were lowered, as the motion was more bearable without the noise aloft and the slamming about and chafing was doing more damage and wearing out the gear faster than any amount of sailing would have done. Every time a whisper of wind came along, those aboard would hopefully rehoist the sails, only to be bitterly disappointed when the wind failed as soon as the mainsail was set.

This was all very tiring and the very smallest marine engine would have given them enough to escape their misery. Although Mr Howells was one of the older type of yachtsmen who considered an engine to be merely a 'stink pot' in a sailing yacht, those two days altered his outlook and he decided to have an engine to combat flat calms in the future.

One hour of this kind of thing was quite enough for us, so we headed for the eastern entrance under engine; although it had been our intention not to put in anywhere until we reached Cherbourg. We went to anchor in the bay and promptly turned in.

About three hours later we were boarded by young customs officer who was the most suspicious and officious one that I have ever met. From the very first moment he came aboard, he treated us not even as if we were suspects but as if we were already proven smugglers. He examined our papers and found them quite in order, but he was not satisfied and sat looking very cunning and pleased with himself, literally grilling us with questions in the manner that he must have seen American detectives assume in gangster films.

He started boasting of his powers as a customs officer.

"Do you know that I can arrest this boat if I want to?" he asked.

We informed him that we were familiar with the powers given to HM Customs, but we could not see why he should ask the question as he already knew that we had only sailed from Brightlingsea.

"How do I know that you have not been across the Channel since you left Brightlingsea?" he snapped back instantly.

We assured him that we did not want to tell him his job but we informed him that a phone call to HM Customs at Brightlingsea would prove to him that we had not had enough time to get there and back.

"But you might have met another boat and trans-ferred dutiable goods," he argued, looking very sly.

That was the first really sensible thing he had said. We told him that if that was what he thought he should go ahead and search, for it was his duty to do so.

Going into Dover Harbour's Eastern Entrance

Then he fired a whole battery of questions at us.

"Why did you come into harbour?"

"Because we were not getting anywhere outside."

"Who did you come into meet?"

"Nobody. We just want a sleep"

"Who was it came out to you after you came in?"

"Nobody, as you probably know. You are the first."

"What time did you get back after going ashore?"

"We have never been ashore, as you can verify by examining our boat. It is still lashed up as it was when we were at sea and its bottom is dry, so it has not been used."

"Why are you going abroad at this time of year?"

By this time we were all fed up to the teeth with his nasty ill-mannered approach and as an answer to his last question, I told him that it was a pretty poor look out when three serving officers could not take their first leave in two years without being treated like defendants in the dock, cross-questioned by the prosecuting counsel.

He fired his last question: "Why are you still waiting in harbour?"

We all four said the same thing: "Because we are waiting for you to get off so that we can sail."

He stepped aboard his launch - still suspicious - and we weighed anchor and motored out while he was watching. Thank goodness, I have always found all the other officers of HM Customs to be the reverse of this unpleasant specimen.

The wind was south westerly when we left Dover but it freshened up into a good sailing breeze later.

That afternoon I had a shocking time. Paul came to me and told me that our WC had gone wrong and, though it had been used, it was not possible to pump it. I had to find out what was amiss with it. For two hours I had the nasty job of pulling the thing to pieces until eventually I found the trouble - a piece of cotton waste which had fallen in and jammed in the pump. Even when I found it, I could not extract it as it was in a very awkward position, but I succeeded in the end by using a brace and bit in the manner of a corkscrew. The whisky that Julian handed to me when I had finished was most welcome, indeed.

That night off Hastings, I turned in leaving Paul and Anthony sailing the yacht which was carrying her second jib, foresail (or more correctly staysail) and mainsail, and making quite good way to windward. Later in the night, I felt that the motion of the yacht was not the same as when I had turned in, so I went on deck and found the watch had set *Topsy's* mizzen and had sheeted it hard home with the result that all the yacht wanted to do was to come up head to wind and heave-to. Only by steering her off wind with the use of the helm was it possible to sail her.

They had imagined that extra sail meant extra speed, which it does when the balance of the sails is correct, but when a lot of helm has to be carried the water pressure on the rudder will slow the boat down. They would have been alright if the big jib had been set.

I was rather cross that they had tried to improve on my orders without consulting me, especially as we had lost ground against a foul tide, but with an agreement that they would not draw their own conclusions and make their own decisions in the future, I again retired with more confidence in them and more sureness of the safety of the vessel. That law was never broken again during the trip.

The next afternoon the wind freshened up and, while we were sailing on the port tack and standing in towards Beachy Head Lighthouse, the gaff jaws broke at the lugs on the gaff which left the mast and jumped into the starboard rigging. I had to go aloft and cut all the ratlines adrift before we could lower the gaff. A large ship which was approaching from the opposite direction avoided us by altering course.

Although they were not seamen, the three Guards officers worked splendidly and we lowered the mainsail without damaging it. Under head sails and mizzen, we reached into Eastbourne pier and anchored in order to take the mainsail off altogether and stow it. When this was done we set a tri-sail on the boom and again sailed out to the position off Beachy Head where we had been when the throat had parted. But we found that the tri-sail was too small to hold the heavy boom out to lee-ward against the rolling of the yacht and, even with the engine to assist us, we had a rough time reaching a position off Seaford Head.

With Newhaven harbour in sight, we were beaten by the tide and on every tack we were being set back inshore towards Beachy Head again. We were all very tired and there was only one thing to do, although it was a very dangerous procedure. We would have to anchor in the worst of all anchorages - an exposed position off a lee-shore.

We anchored and, by gosh, how we rolled! *Topsy* put her rails clean under as she rolled over every large sea and not one loose object down below stayed where it should. We stopped the boom from moving by lowering it until it wedged between the mainsheet horse and the port quarter boards, but we had our work cut out in securing the dinghy and the davits. With everything secured, we turned into our bunks until the tide once more ran to the westward and assisted us to reach and to enter Newhaven.

Topsy takes the rough...

We stopped one day in Newhaven while the local blacksmith repaired the metal gaff jaws and then set sail again towards the west under our full mainsail.

By 1am we were off St Catherine's Point on the Isle of Wight in a really heavy sea but, as the swell was long, *Topsy* took it in her stride. The most uncomfortable thing about that night was continuous rain which blotted out everything. We were abeam of the Needles but well off-shore according to our dead reckoning so we heaved-to and reefed down as the wind had risen to gale force. Then we went into a huddle and debated what we should do. With her second jib aback, the mainsheet slackened off and the helm set hard down *Topsy* needed no attention. It was unanimously agreed that our best course was to heave-to until daylight and then run in through the Needles Channel into the shelter of the Isle of Wight.

This plan was carried out and we entered Yarmouth, where we laid alongside a large yacht, *Le Cygne*. Inspection of the gaff jaws showed them to have bent while we were sailing from Newhaven and, with the help of the Devonshire skipper of *Le Cygne,* we once more straightened the lugs of the gaff. Nobody seemed to know why we were putting such a terrible strain on the throat but I later found that it was because the mainsail had stretched, allowing the throat to go too high up the mast where the gaff placed a great strain on the jaws when it levered itself across the leeward shrouds.

With one reef down, this is not possible and so I had to sail the yacht like that until such time as I was able to get Fred Taylor, the sailmaker of Maldon, to cut the foot of the sail and bring the mainsail once more back to shape and size.

During that day the Yarmouth lifeboat was called out to search for a plane that had been forced down in the Channel but I believe that they were not able to find a trace of the machine.

A very nice-looking yacht of about 15 tons motored in with her large Bermudan mast, broken in three places, towing alongside her. I rather think that she must have been dismasted in the Solent for if such an accident had happened in the seas which we had experienced off the Needles, only cutting everything adrift as quickly as possible would have prevented the broken spars from damaging the sides of the yacht and most probably sinking it.

For two days we sheltered in Yarmouth and then sailed when the wind became north westerly. The Air Ministry's weather forecast predicted strong west winds for sea areas Portland, Wight and Dover, but we were determined to get across so we set a course for Cherbourg. As is so often the case the Air Ministry and the weather were not in agreement, for the wind gradually fined away until, by the time we were just over halfway across the Channel, we were forced to run the little engine to keep way upon the yacht.

We entered Cherbourg next day in a flat calm and tied up opposite the yacht club in the Inner Rade. The last time I had been in Cherbourg, I laid at anchor in HMS *Sluga* in the Outer Rade for nearly three weeks and, because the harbour was chock full of mines of every description and type, I was only able to stretch my legs walking on the detached mole. After looking at the town from that one aspect, I rather wanted to see if from the shoreside but I was very disappointed when I did, for it has nothing to commend it.

As a harbour, though, Cherbourg is good because there is no need, as with most French ports, to heave-to outside for hours awaiting sufficient water to cross the bar.

At a cafe inshore where there was a band, dancing and a cabaret, the proprietress was a typical Madame - very fat and heavily bejewelled. She waddled up to our table and told us in English how good she had been to the American and English soldiers who were in Cherbourg after D-Day and how they had called her Mother. She probably was just as good to the Germans when they were there. Had I been unfortunate to have had a Mother like her, I would have run away from her as soon as I was able to do so.

Out of courtesy the officers bought her a drink and I noticed that the price of her drink came to more than all of ours put together. This went on for a while until Julian went off to have a bath at a hotel and Paul and Anthony went on the floor to dance.

I found myself sitting alone with the old hen. She had already been given a drink by each one of us but she did not attempt to leave our table. My glass was empty so I ordered a bottled beer from the waiter because, although it was not good beer, it certainly was an improvement on the other hooch that they were supplying.

I can understand French well enough to know that Madame told the waiter to inform me in English that there was no more bottled beer. He brought me some kind of expensive spirit that I would not look at and, even worse, brought Madame another of her expensive drinks on my account. I told him that as he had not brought a beer, I did not want a drink and, if I was not drinking, Madame could pay for her own - especially as I had not ordered either drink. If looks could kill, I would have been a dead man.

...and the smooth

I said 'Goodnight' very politely to Madame and left the cafe, returning to the yacht to write some letters home.

Julian returned later in a very dishevelled state and sporting the most beautiful black eye I had seen in years. He had been on his way back to the yacht from his bath when he noticed a commotion going on outside the cafe where we had been and, wondering if Paul and Anthony were mixed up in it, he went to investigate. The next thing he remembers is picking himself up off the ground. Who had hit him and why he was hit, he never found out

The strangest thing about the whole affair was that nearly a dozen gendarmes arrived on bicycles and then stood on the opposite side of the road doing absolutely nothing until the fight wore itself to a standstill. They reminded me of Offenbach's famous old gendarmes duet which begins:

"We're public guardians bold, yet wary, and of ourselves, we take good care."

One day in Cherbourg was enough for all of us and so we decided to push on to Deauville so I did not have a chance to use all my nice new charts of the west coast of France and my new, but pre-war, edition of the Bay of Biscay Pilot Book. It was a dead loss to have purchased them.

When we arrived at Deauville late in the afternoon, it was dead low water and no harbour entrance was visible since everywhere was dried out and the aspect did not correspond with the chart. By easing our way in-shore using the lead we were able to discern through binoculars what, by the position of the Casino, was the entrance. But where a long jetty or pier should have run out, there stood piles only. We waited until slack water at high tide and as it was moonlight and no pilot had come out for us, we chanced our luck and entered, going into what should have been the non-tidal yacht basin. When the tide fell, we discovered that the gates of the basin were missing and we took the ground alongside the quay - thankfully on a soft mud bottom.

All the next day it was absolutely teeming with rain. Paul went along the quay in search of a fresh water hydrant to fill our fresh water tanks and he discovered that the one on the quay alongside where we were lying was the only one in working order but there was no hose available.

We found a piece of hose aboard but it was five feet too short to reach our water filler in the deck so, after putting our largest funnel into the filler, Paul stood on the quay in the pouring rain squirting the fresh water from the hydrant up into the air, aiming it to fall into the funnel. A few moments later there was a terrible to do when a brass bound dock master came tearing along the quay without a raincoat. He began to verbally rip Paul to shreds in French. Julian, who was below with me, listened for a while and then went into fits of laughter, telling us that the dock master was accusing Paul of wasting fresh water by washing the decks down. I have heard of mad dogs and Englishmen going out in the midday sun but never of mad dogs or Englishmen who were mad enough to damp down a yacht's deck during torrential rain.

Paul was no linguist and had no idea why the dock master was raving so much and Julian would not go out enlighten him, so he just carried on guiding the stream of water up into the air and into the funnel. I don't know if it was the realisation that he could not penetrate the stone wall of Paul's silence or the fact that he had become drenched to the skin that made the dock master leave, but he did go away and was not heard of again.

We found Deauville to be the most expensive place we had ever been to and far beyond any of our pockets, so once more we pushed on. We set a course for Le Treport with little expectation of being able to enter but we were fortunate for the wind backed to south and we had a calm sea inshore when we entered at high water.

It was in Le Treport that our fortunes took a turn for the better. We had a comfortable berth afloat in the non-tidal basin and we found the port a nice warm and hospitable place unlike Cherbourg, where we were robbed, or Deauville, where we were fleeced. It was reasonable enough and we voted to stay there awhile.

The stay was worthwhile as we made friends with a French family who were in charge of a racehorse stud farm and the three officers spent an interesting day visiting it. The head of this family had held a high rank in the British Army as a liaison officer and had been awarded the Military Medal sometime during the 1914 war.

The casino on the beach was only a small one but it was comfortable and reasonable and boasted a very good and versatile orchestra. One night we were charged 50 francs extra at the door and found that we had been admitted to a Chamber of Commerce social evening. A very fine evening it was too, with dancing and a long cabaret. The whole affair did not finish until 4am. I have been to France several times since then and I still like Treport as my favourite port while the airs and graces of the millionaires' playground of Deauville are the least in keeping with my character.

Our stay at Le Treport extended to a week or more and then we sailed for Boulogne taking two of our French friends with us for the run. The beginning of the trip was in mist, without any wind, but about ten miles from Boulogne it freshened up as the sun set. As we were entering the harbour under sail, the windward main sheet's leading block strap snapped and the mainsail sheet swept across the cockpit with such violence that it lifted the compass clean up into the air. It fell on to the port rail and then dropped onto the deck where it lay battered and useless. A few seconds earlier one of our guests had been sitting in the cockpit with her back to the main sheet block but she moved just before the mainsheet swept across.

It would have lifted her head off had she stayed where she was sitting for a few moments longer and I still feel hot and cold shivers up the spine

Topsy on the open seas

Overleaf: the wreckage in Boulogne harbour immediately after the war

I think of what might have happened.

Boulogne harbour was a wreck. It had taken a tremendous hammering during the war. We entered in the dark and very slowly motored in after stowing the sails once we were inside the outer breakwater. To find a berth in the dark was pretty hopeless so we tied onto some tall piles near the fishing fleet.

From that moment on we had no rest as the French fishermen have a way of mooring up and coming into the quay that is peculiar to themselves. Those already moored up would be tied by the bow only with just enough slack on the one warp to allow for the large rise and fall of the tide. The next fisherman into harbour would find room for his boat by the simple means of steaming at full speed between two craft already moored, forcing them out on each side until his vessel's bow hit the quay. Then he would hook on with the single warp from the bow and push off ashore. This was repeated every time another boat entered until we were packed like sardines and *Topsy* was hemmed in and squashed. Our only hope of survival was to moor by one rope in the same manner as they did so that we could swing with them, but first we had to remove the bowsprit and bumpkin.

By daylight, we were steaming around looking for a less troublesome berth which we found by lying alongside a filthy old mudhopper.

The main shopping part of Boulogne was still intact as the damage was confined to the areas adjacent to the harbour and to the harbour itself.

Our French guests had a friend in Boulogne and they fetched him back aboard for a drink. He spoke English very well and drank Scotch whisky very well too, all the time he extolling the virtues of his wife who was 'so young, so beautiful, so kind and understanding.' She would never forgive him if we did not go back home with him for supper, he said. So we went.

It was a tidy walk up the hill through the old gateway to his house and we arrived fairly breathless, laughing and joking outside the front door. He rang the bell and was telling us how pleased his wife would be to meet some English friends when the door opened suddenly and we were drenched with water thrown from the darkness of the passage. The door was slammed in

At the Cafe Jules, Boulogne

Opposite: Topsy in Boulogne harbour, hemmed in by the fishing fleet

the Frenchman's face. His wife must have taken us from some of his drinking companions and as he had promised to come home early, she blamed them for keeping him out late. There was a heated dialogue in French between husband and wife through the closed door and eventually she opened it and apologised for throwing water at us. We had a really pleasant evening from then onwards.

To open a packet of English cigarettes in a cafe in Boulogne was a silly thing to do because you would immediately be besieged by everybody and your packet would last no time at all. The only exception was in the Cafe, Jules, which stands in the square. I consider it to be about the best run and cleanest one in the town. The smaller cafes around the back streets are nothing more than dens of sin and iniquity where waitresses and Madame openly twist you out of your change every time you buy a drink.

Our trip home from Boulogne was a wonderful one as, with one reef down, we sailed to the Swin Spitway in under 14 hours without cutting any corners, as we took the Edinburgh, Knock John and Barrow route. Later on, I cut off miles by sailing straight across from the Edinburgh Channels buoy to No10 Barrow.

THE LADY HILDA

Early in 1949 a gentleman from London asked me to take a large yacht from Poole to Burnham-on-Crouch. He had just bought her but he had not had her surveyed before doing so. I told him it was a very silly thing to do but he said he was sure that anything that was wrong with her could be put right by Prior's Yard at Burnham when we got there.

When I looked at her from the quayside I fell in love with her looks. She was a pretty looking vessel. Her gear was set up well and she was fully rigged except for her mizzen mast which lay on the deck in two pieces. The owner told me that the mizzen had been knocked out of her by a ship while she was lying alongside a quay. When I inspected the broken mast I was not surprised. If it had not been knocked out, it would have fallen out anyway as it was in an advanced stage of dry rot. When I saw what was wrong with the mizzen mast it started me thinking, so I looked elsewhere around the ship and I found more dry rot in the deck, under the gratings down aft. She had been laid up with little attention for a very long time.

Below decks she was a picture - well-appointed and beautifully fitted out. She had a very fine and large bathroom but it did appear to me that more money had been spent here than in maintaining her gear in a fit condition for sea.

The yacht had the kind of lines that would catch anyone's eye and she appeared to be the type of vessel that would think little of sailing around the world.

Yes, I had fallen in love with her looks but I thought about that rotten mast and no survey and I could not put much trust in her.

Her gross tonnage was 44 tons and the Thames tonnage 68 tons, the deck length was 78'6", beam 16'6" and draught 10'6". She was rigged the same as *Topsy* but she was a yawl. The yawl rig has a mainmast and a mizzen mast, but the mizzen is fitted astern of the rudder post which gives the yawl a larger mainsail, longer boom and smaller mizzen sail than the ketch, which has the mizzen mast fitted further inboard, ahead of the rudder post.

This yacht had the longest and heaviest solid boom that I have been called upon to handle and I could see that she was a craft that would be hard to work. George Simon, one of my Maldon friends who was a petty officer engineman in minesweepers during the war, went with me as paid crew while the owner and one of his friends came to assist us in sailing the ship round.

The next morning George and I sorted out the sails and made the unhappy discovery that most of them were only for light weather. All of them, with the exception of a new jib, were in a very poor condition and spotted with mildew through being stowed away when they were wet. I found that the mainsail was seam sick along the foot so I cut out the use of that part of the sail by taking in a reef. I had to stitch up any other seams which I found to be in a similar condition and I spent the better part of the day with a palm and needle while George and the owner worked on the engine.

In order to fill the freshwater tanks we had to move the yacht across the river to a berth alongside Poole Quay and in moving the *Lady*, as I came to call her, I had my first shock.

The wind was fresh from the south west, so to get away from our berth I had only to let go the lead lines and wait for the bows to blow out towards the centre of the river. When the yacht's head was in the position I required, I let go the aft warps and rang 'Slow ahead'. Immediately the engine was put into gear, the yacht started to turn rapidly to starboard and, although I put the wheel hard to port, she still turned up wind trying to put her enormous bowsprit onto the quay. All I could do was ring down 'Stop'. As soon as the screw stopped revolving, the yacht turned back to port again but each time I went ahead she would turn rapidly to starboard. I soon became fed up with this. Anyone on the quay must have thought I was daft to be handling a yacht in such a strange way, so I just let the yacht blow across the river to Poole Quay and then went in search of a reason for this strange behaviour.

I discovered that the yacht was fitted with one engine on the port side only, which would not have affected steering of the ship too badly if it had been fitted so that her propeller shaft ran parallel to the keel and the screw came somewhere well aft. But in this case the engine was fitted amidships and the propshaft stuck out the side of the vessel.

She would be a beast to handle in confined spaces but, as she was lying port side to the quay, the tendency to turn to starboard would actually help me in getting away on this occasion and once she was moving the action of the rudder would take charge and keep her straight.

The next afternoon the wind eased away to a moderate south westerly so we left Poole under the engine as far as the Bar Buoy where we set the sails. Setting the mainsail was a four man job and we were all very breathless by the time we had finished and had paid the yacht's head off onto our course for St Catherine's Point. Before we passed the Needles, our moderate south west wind had increased to half a gale and from time to time we were lashed by rain squalls. Off St Catherine's Point we were running with a heavy sea on the starboard quarter but the motion of the yacht was very good - except for one thing. She simply would not stay on her course for 15 seconds at a time and she needed constant steering and attention.

From St Catherine's Point to the Nab Tower was a bit naughty and the owner was not feeling too well. His friend had already given up and retired below after being very seasick. I seemed unable to get past the Nab Tower because we simply did not have enough speed to beat the tide as the bottom of the yacht was very foul with weed. The weather was getting worse and I wanted to get the yacht into the anchorage in the lee of the Isle of Wight at St Helen's Bay.

George and the owner started the engine but it stopped as soon as they switched it over from petrol to paraffin. I had to sail the yacht alone while they cleaned all the fuel pipes, filters, jets and carburetters - no mean job on a Kelvin four-cylinder marine engine in a heavy sea. Although we had a barrel of paraffin vaporising oil, we could not use

The Lady Hilda. She had the kind of lines that would catch anyone's eye

it as the paraffin fuel tank was rusty and the rust choked the fuel pipe lines. We were very short of petrol and we did not have enough to reach the anchorage while we were punching against the tide, so we had to stop the engine in order to save the last two gallons for starting up if we eventually able to clean out the paraffin tank.

North of the fairway, we handed the head sails and anchored with the mainsail set as we would have drifted to hell and gone in the time it would take three of us to get the mainsail down and stowed.

When we did start to lower the mainsail, the fun began. The yacht was fitted with two topping lifts, one each side of the sail, and we had the devil's own job to make that heavy and wet flax sail run down between them. As the boom had to clear a deck house fitted amidships, it could not be lowered more than level with the crown of my head and as both George and the owner were short men, it was an impossibility to stow the sail on the boom in the conditions we were working in. Then the main sheet arrangement did not sheet in the boom enough to stop the heavy boom from slamming from side to side so we had to duck our heads each time it swung across. Once I forgot and received a crack on the head which laid me *hors de combat* for a while. We did get the mainsail down but it was not furled - simply lashed up enough at intervals to stop it from blowing to pieces in the wind. The gallows were set up under the boom after a great struggle and the boom was lashed up each way to stop any movement.

That night at anchor was anything but comfortable and at dawn, when the tide was favourable, we used our last two gallons of petrol to motor into the big ship anchorage off St Helen's. There we anchored once again. We were now totally out of petrol and we would not be able to start the engine again, even if we did clean the paraffin fuel tank now that we were in a quieter anchorage.

The owner and his friend had experienced quite enough of the sea for a while and wanted to get ashore, but for most of the day we had no means of getting them off until at about 3pm a Naval MFV (Motor Fishing Vessel) under the command of a RNVR lieutenant came near enough for us to hail him and, on his return to Portsmouth Harbour, he took the owner and his friend with him.

George and I, now alone aboard the yacht, spent a fairly comfortable night. Our friend the MFV came out again next morning and paused long enough to tell us that the owner had arranged to have petrol sent out to us and that he had just received a gale warning from Portsmouth Command: 'Severe north west gale. Imminent'. If this was the case and the wind changed to north west, we would be anchored off a lee-shore. As the tide was in our favour, George and I weighed anchor and, with our big jib only, we sailed the yacht into Spithead where we anchored near to a large Naval sloop that was engaged on radar experiments. The gale warning was correct. At the change of tide the wind veered into the north west and piped up as bad a blow as I can remember in those waters.

Aboard the yacht it was plain misery. Often she put her bowsprit right under a sea before lifting and there were times when she took seas over her bows. The rolling was so violent that the chairs in the saloon tumbled about like acrobats and, as the boom seemed to want to join in the dance, we doubled all its securing lashings. The worst thing of all was the sound of a lot of water under the floors slooshing from side to side and bringing up at the end of each roll against something with a crash that shook the whole yacht. George and I lifted the floorboards and discovered that there was a lot of water under the floors forward and midships. The yacht was leaking badly somewhere.

A large fresh water tank holding about four tons of water was fitted under the saloon floor and this was where the sound of surging water, the mighty crashing and the shaking came from. It was obvious that this tank was leaking, too, because a full tank cannot surge and it had been filled up in Poole and not used since. If the tank had ever had any baffles in it, it was patent that they had carried away or the water could never have surged so much.

George and I manned the pump and for hour after hour we worked that pump handle up and down, turn and turn about. We at least did make some impression on the level of water under the floors.

We then made it a practice to have half an hour's nap each and while one slept the other stayed on watch, working the pump from time to time. But before long we both received the shock of our lives. I had gone below to call George for his watch and during a sudden violent gust of wind, our anchor cable started to run out over the gypsy of the winch. George and I could not get up onto the deck fast enough.

The cable stopped for a few seconds and then as we arrived at the winch it started running out again - so fast that it showered sparks as it jumped the webs of the gypsy. Then suddenly it jammed when a shackle reached the webs. The cable was not the correct size for the gypsy of the winch. We now had five shackles, or 75 fathoms, of cable out and our little CQR anchor was holding in a wonderful way. We did the best we could to pass a stopper on the cable and, thank goodness, it held during the next heavy squall.

"What happens if that cable runs right out?" George asked.

"We will most probably end up on the submarine barrier that runs from the fort to the land," I answered. "Unless we could set the jib in time and were able to steer through the gateway between the forts, that old foresail would never stand this wind."

"I'm going to have a look at that engine," said George. "They may get some petrol out to us."

"You must be a first prize optimist if you really think so," I answered. "There is not a hope in China while it blows like this."

Soon a new danger threatened when the large sloop ahead of us which was riding two anchors started to drag down onto us. Her crew paid out more anchor cable but still she dragged until she missed us by something like 50 yards. They weighed anchor and then, of all the silly things to do, they steamed up wind and re-anchored in the same spot. I told George that I though that it was a bloody silly thing to do because as she had dragged her anchors once, she could certainly do so again and next time she might not miss us. If she did hit us in that sea, she would certainly sink us.

With this in mind, I kept watch sitting in the shelter of the deck house and at about 4am the sloop appeared to be very much nearer than she had been. I signalled to her bridge with a torch and asked: "Are you dragging?"

The answer came back: "Have not since last night."

My signal must have raised doubts in the mind of the officer of the watch, though, and he must have checked his bearings and found that his ship had moved from her original position. Within a few minutes of the signals, her commanding officer was on the bridge. By dawn she was in such a position that had she swung her stern towards us she would have hit us.

That she did not, we owe entirely to the seamanship of the commanding officer. With her twin screws, he held the ship with her stern away from us while the crew on the ship's head weighed the starboard anchor. Then he signalled to pay out more cable on the port anchor until there was enough paid out to enable him to lie to the one anchor without the risk of hitting us. By this time his ship's bows were astern of us. The sloop dragged the single anchor very quickly and very soon she was sufficiently astern of us for the anchor to be weighed. The sloop then steamed off into Portsmouth harbour leaving us alone in Spithead.

One very great danger had been removed but with its passing we suddenly felt very lonely anchored out there by ourselves. But by that afternoon, my remark to George that there was not a hope in China of the petrol being brought out to us proved to be incorrect.

The wind died down with the ebb tide until it became a fresh west north westerly but there was still a fairly bad sea running, although not so inhumanly vicious as the one we had already experienced. George was working at the bilge pump while I was down below when I heard him shout excitedly: "There's a boat coming out."

I went on deck to have a look. As it approached us it threw spray all over itself, meeting every wave. It looked something like a lifeboat coming out, but, as it came nearer to us, I could see that it was a motor boat of about 25 feet in length with a covered-in bow. It was making really splendid way through the rough sea. I could see two men in the craft dressed in oilskins and sou'westers. I was never more pleased to see anyone than I was that day to see Mr Butcher from the Camber in Portsmouth harbour. I admired his pluck in coming out to us with fuel on a day like that and George and I were hardly able to tell him how very grateful we were.

Steering his boat alongside us but keeping about 40 feet away, he hailed us.

"We have some petrol for you, throw us a line and we will hang onto your stern."

With his launch dancing about on the end of a rope astern of us, we ferried the five gallon drums across on a long rope and then the launch pushed off back into harbour.

The back of the gale had been broken and the sky indicated better weather on the way. George spent the day cleaning all the pipe lines and the two fuel tanks while I persisted with the everlasting pumping, but I never did pump that bilge dry.

With everything ready, George prepared to start up the engine and we both had happy visions of harbour, rest and food, but we were not to realise them that day. Would that engine start? Would it, heck. George sweated and swore but could not get one bang out of it.

The weather was fining away nicely but still we were stuck in Spithead. George by now was using really lurid language and had come to the conclusion that the points of the magneto were dirty but we had no magneto file or anything with which to clean them. Thoroughly exhausted with our efforts to start the engine and the prolonged pumping to lower the water sufficiently to enable us to have a few hours rest, we turned in and slept like the dead. The gale, bilge pumps and engine could not have troubled us less.

When we went on deck next morning we found that the sun was shining, the sea was calm and life had once more appeared in Spithead. We had breakfast and then started on the first job, pumping to get the water in the bilge down to a reasonable level.

While we were doing this, a customs launch came alongside and the officer aboard told us that the Spit Sand Fort had informed them that we had been doing a lot of pumping during the gale. He had phoned Southampton and been told that, if he thought it was necessary, he was to stop the yacht from going on further for safety reasons.

Enjoying the calm

This would never do as we had to get to Burnham within the next two days because I had a job booked for my own yacht. Somehow I had to stall him off, so I told him that I did not think the yacht was making very much water but that the four tons of fresh water in the main tank was leaking into the bilge. He seemed satisfied with my explanation, especially when I added that the yacht would be taken into harbour as soon as we could start the engine and that some work would be done at Camper and Nicholson's yard in Gosport.

The customs officer also informed us that a tug was coming out to tow us in. This was bad news too because I did not think that the owner had realised how much it would cost him. If we were unable to move and handle ourselves and we accepted the tow, we might be claimed as salvage. Our one hope was to get the engine running and, if we could only steer, we would not be salvage.

George had another go at it. The previous night the engine mixture must have become too rich for the weak spark of the magneto, because that morning it started straight away. We did not dare stop it again but kept it running on petrol, in neutral, all the time we were weighing anchor. It took us nearly an hour to wind in the cable for although we had five shackles of cable out, it was more like seven shackles that had to be wound in because the part of the cable that did not fit the gypsy would jump the webs and run out again every now and again.

At last we were under way and we met Frazer and White's tug as we were passing Southsea Castle. When the skipper hailed us, I refused his assistance and we entered harbour under our own steam to tie up alongside the old *Zara* on Camper and Nicholson's mooring at Gosport.

I phoned the owner who told me to leave the yacht for a while until he could see to the engine, so I went home by train in order to do my trip with *Topsy* while George stayed aboard to look after the yacht.

Work was carried out on the *Lady* during the next fortnight and then I returned to her and ran her round to Burnham-on-Crouch by engine as we had a flat calm sea and no wind for most of the way. The yacht had been difficult to steer while under sail, but that was nothing compared to the way in which she steered under engine only. If the steering wheel was moved more than three spokes either way of amidships, she would take a sheer off her course and try to turn right round. She positively wore us out trying to keep her straight.

We arrived at Burnham without more trouble and handed the yacht over to Prior's boatyard for stripping and to have everything done to her that was necessary.

Later on in the season I saw Reg Prior and he said to me: "Go and look at the yacht's main mast lying in my yard."

"Why?" I asked him.

"You need to ask why?" retorted Reg. "We're fitting her with a new one. The old one has no more than about a quarter of an inch of solid wood in it from the hounds to the mast head. You would never have brought her round if you had known that it was like that and I cannot see how you didn't roll it out of her when you were at anchor in the gale."

Opposite: Burnham-on-Crouch

I inspected the mainmast and found it was indeed in the same condition as the mizzen mast had been.

I told George that if I ever saw the *Lady* again it would be too soon for me, but my words were a little premature. I was to see her again and cure her little game of being hardheaded. It was later the same year when the owner asked me to take the renovated *Lady Hilda* to Holland.

On this particular journey we filled the domestic tank with fresh water but left the four ton water tank under the saloon floor empty. As soon as we sailed, the difference in the yacht could be felt. She danced and curtsied over every wave and her bows were so buoyant that she gave me the feeling she would always rise to a sea. I had much more confidence in her this time. The large water tank under the saloon floor must have been an addition to the yacht since she was designed - probably added to give a good water supply for her luxurious bathroom - but when it was full, it placed ballast too far forward and altered the trim of the yacht. We had laid the bogey that caused the yacht to handle so badly.

In the future, I decided, the owner must fill the aft water tank only and then he would have a large yacht that would steer as easily as a dinghy. From being the hardest headed and worst steering yacht I had ever handled, the *Lady* became as meek and tractable as a kitten.

A SINKING OFF KENT

I n 1948 Derek Harvey, an ex RAF type, had paid me to move two landing craft assault vessels and three jolly boats from Gillingham to Maldon. LCAs were used for landing on the beaches of the Normandy coast on D Day. They are flat-bottomed boats with a landing ramp at the bow and the two LCAs that I fetched round were powered by twin Ford V8 engines.

We had a little trouble with the one that we were towing because her ramp on the bow was so distorted that it would not fit sufficiently well to keep out the sea if it was anything more than a flat calm. But the weather was very good to us and we got round without much trouble.

Derek removed the damaged ramp and boarded the bow up with tongue and groove timber. The vessel became his home after he had a cabin fitted by Webb and Feesey at Maldon.

In 1949, about six weeks after I had fetched the *Lady* round from Poole, Derek asked me if I would take his boats round to the Hamble river for him. The engines of the LCA were running very sweetly and we decided to tow the houseboat with the workboat. I left Derek to purchase enough rope for the tow line and to get the boats ready for sea, as I was busy elsewhere.

Derek came to me later and told me that his partner owned a Falmouth quay punt and as he was moving to the Hamble with Derek, he would like his small yacht towed round at the same time.

I did not see the yacht until she was brought out to us off Heybridge Basin as we were about to start the trip. If I had seen it earlier, I would never have taken her. My first sight of her was when her owner, Len Carrick, rowed out to us. I was sure she would never reach the Hamble as her topsides were well opened by lying so long in the canal. Her mast was not stepped but was lashed on the deck and, although Len had carried out a lot of work aboard her, she still had a lot that needed doing before she would be fit for sea.

Len was a shipwright and assured me that she was better than she looked, so I took her in tow astern of the second LCA.

It was a fine day when we started and the wind was a moderate south west but I soon found that Derek had not bought a tow rope either strong enough or long enough. It parted when we were off Jaywick, leaving the quay punt adrift, and I had to put about to pick her up again. We used whatever suitable rope we could find aboard the workboat to lengthen the tow. Len went aboard his yacht and baled her out while we were doing this.

This interlude messed us about and delayed us enough to put miles and hours onto our course. I was going to cut through the Swin Spitway, but when we arrived at the Wallst buoy there was too little water for the quay punt and we had to go right round the Gunfleet Sands. I still hoped to cut one corner through the Golmer Gat but as we were unable to steam at more than half speed without the tow rope pulling up taut, we did not arrive at the Gat until it was pitch dark and low water. I was not prepared to chance the short cut in those conditions, so we plugged on to the NE Gunfleet, making only two knots.

When we turned into the Barrow Deeps we were with the tide but against the wind which meant a considerable swell and I learned how uncomfortable an LCA can be. They hit a swell with their square bows making a loud thudding noise and they pound badly. Whenever spray was thrown up by the bows it was whipped by the wind through the whole length of the boat. In the workboat we had a half-built wheelhouse with no glass in the windows, but we stretched a tarpaulin across to act as a dodger and we were fairly comfortable behind it.

We had passed the old Gunfleet Lighthouse on the starboard hand and were approaching a wreck on the port side when the ebb set down the Barrow Deeps and brought us almost to a standstill. An hour later, as dawn broke, we could see our tow. The houseboat was riding well and following straight astern of us and I turned a little off my course in order to bring the yacht into view

"Well, Len, she's still there. We haven't lost her in the night," I said.

"Yes, she's riding well. Look how high her bow is. I guess that there can't be much water in her," Len replied. "I'm going to light the Primus for a cup of coffee."

He was only inside the workshop for a minute or so and then he returned to ask me for a match. As he waited for me to find a box in my pocket, he

looked over my shoulder and shouted: "Look at my boat, she's sinking!"
"My God, so she is," I answered.

The yacht was acting like a vessel does when she is down by the head,
sheering first one way and then the other with a slow sickening roll.

I put the engines of the towing boat in neutral and, as the cabins of the
two LCAs held more wind than the low lying yacht, the two boats blew
back onto the yacht. With buckets in their hands, Derek and Len reached
the yacht by way of the houseboat. This was almost suicidal as Derek had
constructed the cabin tops of the two LCAs with only about six inches of
decking along their sides and he had not fitted any hand rails on the tops of
the cabins. There was nothing to hold
onto and because of the way an LCA
will roll when abeam to a sea, it is a
wonder to me that they made it to the
yacht without being thrown over the
side.

They started to bale out for dear
life, as quickly as they could handle
the buckets, while the three boats
drifted rapidly with the wind and tide.
I could judge by our drift that we
would find ourselves back over the
wreck that we had passed some time
before and I had visions of our tow
ropes sagging below water and hold-
ing us fast to it. I decided to let go of our anchor. It was then that I discovered that the workboat had only one shackle of cable -15 fathoms - and that
it was insufficient for the anchor to hold.

*Cold comfort aboard
an LCA*

By now the yacht had drifted into a position between the workboat and
the houseboat and as I stood looking at her I could see that she was settling
down bodily very rapidly. There was no chance to do anything about her
and I shouted to the two men to pull the houseboat, which was about six
yards away from them, towards them and get aboard of it while they were
able to. When they realised that the yacht was indeed on its way down,
both men stood as if paralysed, then Len snapped out of it and threw off his
jacket, kicked off trousers and shoes and dived overboard. Derek stood
still as the yacht kicked up her stern in the air and slid beneath the surface
leaving him swimming.

I knew that it was not possible for any man to swim to me against the
tide that was running, even though our anchor was dragging, and I was
preparing to slip both the anchor cable and the tow rope to the houseboat
in order to leave me free to handle the workboat round to pick them up

when a very strange thing happened.

I saw Derek, who was swimming with a slow breast stroke, coming towards me at a terrific speed and as he came up to the stern of the workboat I pulled him aboard. The houseboat came towards us bows first for a second or two and then it spun rapidly right round and charged at us at an alarming rate, stern first. I saw Len alongside our port quarter and I was reaching over to pull him aboard when the stern of the houseboat hit on the same side with a mighty crash. Len was only just in time to sink below the surface before the two boats met. Another two seconds and his head would have been squashed flat. He surfaced about two yards away from us and swam to us so that Derek and I were able to pull him aboard.

What had happened was that as the yacht sank, she had caught the tow rope between the two LCAs with her short bowsprit and her weight pulled the first LCA. back to the spot where she had disappeared, enabling me to reach Derek. Then the tow rope came clean and the yacht continued her dive to the bottom in twelve fathoms of water. This, in turn, tightened up the tow rope rope from the yacht to the stern of the houseboat, making the houseboat spin round and charge us stern first.

Thank God both the men were back aboard the first LCA safely and nobody had been drowned, but we were still in a fix as the anchor was down and we were also fast by a tow rope to a wreck. The wind and tide caused the houseboat to drag her anchor until we were lying stern first to the towed LCA, anchored to the sunken yacht by her tow rope.

Lying in this fashion gave me a chance to attend to the two men, who were dripping with water and shivering. Len now owned no more clothes than those in which he stood, namely one singlet, a pair of pants and a pair of socks. Derek was wet through and all his clothes were aboard the houseboat. Luckily for Derek he had left his duffle coat aboard the workboat when he and Len went aboard the yacht. I gave Len my duffle coat and seaboot stockings while Derek shivered naked under his duffle coat.

My first job was to warm them up and I accomplished this by making them a pint of hot coffee each. Len was suffering from the shock of losing his yacht and for a short while he talked very wildly, but later he calmed down and took his losses like a man.

I very much admired the way he could do it as poor Len had lost everything in the world that he had possessed. Aboard his yacht he had placed all his tools, best clothes and personal belongings and, on top of everything, the yacht was not insured. His money, ration cards and his identification card were in his wallet in the jacket he had cast off as the yacht sank. This was the second time in Len's life that this had happened. He lost all his personal belongings when the ship he was serving in during the war was sunk by a torpedo.

As soon as the men had stopped shivering with cold and shock, we discussed the position and the reasons why the yacht had sunk so suddenly. One feasible explanation was that the yacht may have hit a floating bulk of timber that the other craft had just missed and that she had stoved in a plank on her bow. The second probable reason was that the yacht had lain for two years or more in the canal at Heybridge Basin and the fresh water of the canal is none too good for a softwood boat. She may have become nail sick and started a butt whilst punching into a head sea.

The third reason for sinking I consider to be the most likely. Len had removed the engine but he had left the propeller shaft screw still in place. He had also removed the rudder so that there was nothing except the coupling fitted on the end of the shaft to stop it from working right out of the stern tube. This could not happen if the coupling was a tight fit and secured, but Len was unable to say for certain if it was. If the shaft had worked out of the stern tube, it would have been like filling the yacht with water from a pressure pump with a one inch nozzle. Then, as she settled lower in the water, the topsides that had opened would increase the speed of the inrush of the sea. Still, she had gone and nobody would ever know the reason why.

Topsy at anchor

The problem of getting free from the sunken yacht solved itself. The tow line from the stern of the second LCA to the yacht was now as taut as it could be and, as the LCA yawed about with the tide and rose to a swell, the line was subjected to a great strain. On one large swell the strain became greater than the breaking strain of the rope and it parted, leaving us lying to our anchor only.

The workboat had a two or three foot long split along her port side near to the transom where the stern of the houseboat had struck it, but as it was not lined or panelled out it was a simple matter for us to stop up the leak with cloth from the inside. We could not tell what damage the second LCA had sustained and we decided to push on to Margate where we could put the two boats on the mud for inspections and repairs.

We reached Margate without any trouble as our speed was greatly increased now that we had two vessels of the same type and no small yacht to worry about. After we had tied up, we reported the loss of the yacht to the coastguard who phoned the position of the wreck through to Dover. Len, who was now dressed in Derek's clothes that had been aboard the houseboat, obtained emergency cards with the aid of the Custom's written word that he had lost his identification card at sea. Derek purchased a new tow rope that was long enough and strong enough for the job.

The damage to the stern of the houseboat was serious enough but it was confined to above the water line. So great had been the impact between the two vessels that the socket and the top of the port rudder had been driven right through the transom. Both boats were repaired as well as we could do it and we pushed on for the Hamble river.

We arrived at Gosport without too much difficulty, where I had to leave Derek and Len and return home for another booking. Len and Derek could take the boats the rest of the distance through the Solent whenever they had a calm day. We had overstepped our time margin due both to the sinking and to the reduced speed that was required because of the condition of the repaired boats.

I have been in all kinds of boats in various states of sea, but I have never met a motion the equal of LCAs. As you stand at the wheel and look along the craft towards the bow, you can see the bow twist one way while the stern where you are standing is twisting the opposite way. The cabin top was nice and tight when we started but woodwork cannot stand wracking to that degree and it was soon showing daylight through the seams.

Olive and I had married a fortnight before this trip in the LCAs and we had bought a small general stores in Maldon where we had made our home.

When I arrived home I was greeted by Olive with the order: "You are not to take any more of other people's old crocks about. Stick to *Topsy* in the future."

That is all very well, but living expenses being what they are these days, I am not in a position to refuse taking any boat around the coast that has a reasonable expectation of being able to reach its destination.

Variety is the spice of life and you get plenty of variety running other people's boats.

THE BIG FREEZE

That winter of 1948/49 the River Blackwater was not navigable as it had frozen up nearly solid. It had been a long time since there was such a severe freeze up and I, myself, have never seen the river as it was for those six weeks. Wal Pitt told me that years ago it was worse and that he was able to skate up the river to Chelmsford and that a bonfire had been lit on the ice at Fullbridge, near to John Sadd's timber yards.

The beginning of a freeze-up is the most dangerous time for any yacht at anchor because the ice is very thin then and it is as sharp as a razor. On the flood tide when the river froze, *Topsy* was at anchor and she can still show the scars on her stem at the waterline where the ice cut her before there was enough water for me to move her to the quay.

During such a freeze-up some years ago, two fishermen left their smack at anchor down by Southey rather than risk steaming up through the thin ice. They went ashore by punt and walked home, thinking that the smack would come to less harm down where they had left her rather than higher up the reaches. But when they returned for her, they found that only her mast was above water because the sharp ice grinding along her water line in the same place throughout the ebb tide had cut clean through her planking until she filled and sank. She was eventually lifted and salvaged by the barge *Salcote Belle*.

Later, when the ice became thick and heavy, it was a picture to watch it on the flood tide or for one hour of the ebb. Very large floes floated up the river, sliding one on top of another whenever they found obstruction to their passage and piling up into a solid mass in the bends of the river. The

Overleaf: the Maldon fishermen, iced in for six weeks. They include Sam and Kelly Wright (in punt), Gus Saunders, Arthur Wright and Charlie Pitt(on shore), Reg and Arthur Pitt (on smack) and Alf Pitt (in dinghy)

air was filled with cracking like pistol shots.

The fishermen protected their smacks by hanging oyster dredges, anchors and cables over the side. This has the effect of restricting the movement of ice along the side of the boats and prevents the scoring that would otherwise take place.

Throughout the cold spell I had a fire going aboard the yacht and I had to make excursions down to her every four hours in order to keep it going. The noise made by the ice alongside when you heard it down below deck was rather frightening and the timbers groaned when the pressure of a jam in the centre of the fairway forced the yacht hard up against the quay. I thought that she would sustain serious damage but a series of circumstances saved her.

Firstly, there were two barges lying alongside the quay ahead of *Topsy* and on the ebb tide they diverted most of the moving ice, leaving a frozen area that was stationary between the yacht and the barges. Secondly, a two inch off-mooring wire stretched from the barge *Leonard Piper* lying on blocks astern of the yacht succeeded in holding back the very large floes, cutting through them like a grocer's wire through cheese. The strain on that wire was so great that it quivered and sang but it never parted. Thirdly, I copied the fishermen and hung every available piece of heavy metal over the side.

There was plenty of ice around *Topsy* and I walked on it several times when I inspected her sides, but it moved only slowly and was very thick so that it caused little damage except for pulling every bit of stopping out of the bottom of the yacht and removing all traces of paint.

Two barges were trapped at anchor further down the river and the skippers and mates would walk ashore to get a pint.

One of the minesweepers in the mud berths at Heybridge Basin broke adrift with the pressure of ice and was carried up the Basin Reach to a position midway between the Point and Ladywood, which is the south west end of Northey Island. Surprisingly she sustained little damage.

About 3 o'clock one morning while I was lying in my bed at home I heard the sound of water breaking like waves on the shore during an onshore gale, so I dressed and went down to the Hythe Quay to investigate. I was amazed to find the river in a most turbulent mood. In the centre of the river the ice had been washed aside and quite large white crested waves were tearing down like a bore. It was an extraordinary sight in the moonlight. It was unusual, to say the least, and more so as the tide was flooding up. I wondered why the river was acting in this unexpected manner and could think of no solution.

In actual fact, the weir at Beeleigh had given way under the strain of flood water and ice so that all the water in the Chelmer Canal was emptying itself into the River Blackwater. This had the effect of denuding Heybridge Basin of water and all the yachts and houseboats which normally stayed afloat all the year round took the ground, lying about at every conceivable angle. When water could once more be held in the canal, many of the old houseboats failed to rise and stayed down with only their cabin tops showing above water.

All work came to a standstill for six weeks and, except for keeping an eye on *Topsy's* welfare, I had nothing to do. Not that I would have been pleased if I had needed to go to sea for I am no lover of bitterly cold weather, but I felt very sorry for the fishermen who live from day to day by the fruits of their labours as they were reduced to wildfowling from the islands and saltings which can be reached at low water if you are wearing sea boots. Their chances of earning a living by oyster dredging would be reduced to nil for two seasons to come.

When the thaw set in and the ice disappeared down river, it left the river bed in a very clean condition and it deepened the channel over by the saltings by cutting

Willing hands

the mud down as straight as the sides of a house, but many tree trunks roots littered the bottom. For three months, I was able to sail *Topsy* away from the quay on any high water but after that my berth silted up again and I am now only able to move the yacht on high water spring tides.

In the spring I registered the yacht as a fishing smack and purchased a fish trawl to try my luck at trawling, but I found that it was a poor paying task except for the short time that soles were in the river or estuary. Since the war, fewer and fewer good class fish have been coming in and the local fishermen have not troubled very much about trawling. They have concentrated instead on gathering oysters and winkles.

Finding that fish trawling in this area did not pay, I purchased a shrimp trawl and installed a boiler for cooking the shrimps. For a while I did very well. When I first sailed down the river with the intention of shrimping, the local fishermen told me that I was two or three weeks too early for the shrimps to be there, but I had a shot in the Stone Bight and on my first haul I found that I had as many shrimps as I could handle in the boiler at one time. I returned to the quay with 20 or 30 gallons of shrimps after working one low tide. Being the first in the field I had no trouble at all in finding a local market so I really went at it for three weeks.

I found shrimping could be interesting and the smell of freshly cooked shrimps drying on the trays always made me feel hungry so that my appetite became enormous. Olive signed on as cook and I employed one hand to help me with the trawl. After the trawls had been hauled aboard there would be no rest and, while Olive steered the boat back up tide, the hand and I would empty the contents of the trawl on deck and prepare the net for going over the side again.

By the time we had thrown all weed and dozens of crabs over the side and put our catch in the boiler which contained salt water with more salt added, Olive would have steered the boat back to where we once more streamed the trawl. The shrimps would be cooked and put on the drying racks just in time for the second haul and so the routine would be repeated until about one hour's flood after which we would jog slowly up the river to arrive at Maldon with just enough water to float us.

The manner of paying Olive, the hand and myself was to divide the money received for the catch to one share each and one for the ship. I found that no smell was left in the yacht because of the cooking and that if the decks were thoroughly cleaned down when we had finished, no-one could have told that it had been used for trawling.

After the local shrimpers, 'Tablo' Pitt and his sons in *Tiny Mite,* and the Tollesbury shrimpers started, I found that it was an increasingly difficult task to sell my catch, so I left them to their shrimping and concentrated on re-fitting *Topsy* for cruising.

No matter how many times one has been up and down the river it never seems to become boring, for each Essex waterway has a fascination of its own. To my way of thinking the Dutch waterways are dull and uninteresting in comparison. For eighty percent of the time in Holland it is only possible to see the not very picturesque dykes and, perhaps, the roof of a church - only the never ending stream of traffic holds any interest. But the Essex rivers run through land that is above water level and one's view is not restricted to a winding and well buoyed waterway weaving through mud banks.

I can imagine nothing more peaceful and soothing than to lie at anchor in the Barnacle at Osea Island on a calm evening. All the cares and noises of the world are very far removed from the serenity felt aboard the yacht when only the tide gurgling around the anchor cable and the bows and the cry of the curlew and other wild birds disturbs the quietness. That sense of peace must have existed since the days when the Essex rivers first came into existence and the earlier boatmen must have felt it exactly as I can feel it today.

Getting under way at dawn has an atmosphere of its own. The first herald of dawn - the first moving object just before it is light - is a seagull silently wheeling off to start his day doing whatsoever business seagulls carry out. The air is fresh and cold and there is a mist around us. What water can be seen from the yacht is as still as a mirror. The clanking of the pawl on our windlass sounds loudly and rings out clearly and crisply, echoing from some building ashore.

Through the mist there comes to us the sound of voices with every word reaching us as clearly as if the speaker was aboard us.

"Keep a look out to starboard, Fred. I saw a yacht brought up in the Barnacle last night. We should be near her now."

Out of the mist a barge emerges. She has every stitch of canvas set but her sails are hanging limply and only lifting now and again as a light draught of air fills them, giving her just enough steerage way to enable her skipper to work her up with the tide. A cheery hail of "Morning" and her skipper hauls her off a little to port. He has fixed his position by us and is heading up for the Doctor buoy.

Nobody in the world can beat these sailing bargemasters at this kind of thing. I sometimes think that they must be about the most patient men on earth - at least those who have no engine to help them on their way. The skipper is not worried. He will work her up to the point slowly but surely, and Mr Wright, the water bailiff will take him in tow with his motor launch from there to Fullbridge. The few barges that still ply this river are all that remains of a commercial life in the upper reaches, although Danish eel boats come to Heybridge Basin.

Olive signed on as cook when Topsy became a shrimper

Fifty years ago the River Blackwater and Maldon were hives of industry but the coming of the railway killed the river trade and lately the water has silted up to the point where it is rapidly declining into a trickle of shallow water running between extensive mud banks, thanks to neglect, inattention and pollution.

If the small amount of traffic carrying timber to John Sadd's yard and flour to the mills at Fullbridge ceases altogether, the upper reaches of the River Blackwater will die and become merely the playground of a few small pleasure boats and dinghies. The Dutch would never have wasted such an asset as this river in the way that has been done here in the past years.

Many times I have listened to the older locals arguing the pros and cons of this subject and they become very bitter about it. They will tell how the Admiralty, during the 1914 war, wanted to shut off the river with lock gates after dredging and how the authorities, whoever they may have been, turned the proposal down with the question: "Who is going to pay for the upkeep of the gates after the war has finished?"

The old timers maintain that as it would have become the largest and safest sheet of water in the whole of the Thames estuary, the mooring fees for yachts and boats, together with the business brought to the town, would have paid for the gates hundreds of times over. Burnham-on-Crouch would not have been able to approach Maldon as an anchorage for fair size yachts as the Crouch suffers from a fairly strong tide, is somewhat exposed and is congested with moorings. Again the old timers will moan of how a dredging firm offered to dredge the river and, in return, wanted to keep the ballast they extracted and how the offer was withdrawn after the authorities demanded threepence per ton for the ballast on top of having the work done for them free of charge. Today, it is possible to walk across the river at low water but the elder fishermen will tell how they were able to leave their smacks afloat at anchor in the Bath Hole once upon a time.

I am no authority on dredging and I am only passing on the remarks I have had made to me by men who were here years before I came. They are not necessarily my opinions, but when I survey the river at low water, I do feel that the Dutch have forgotten more about the way to maintain a waterway at its maximum efficiency then we in England have ever known.

It was during this spring of 1949 that my old sleeve valve Kelvin engine gave up the ghost altogether. One very dark and dirty night I started the engine while lying at anchor off Osea Island and it suddenly raced away at a terrific speed when it was still in neutral and then, with a mighty crash, it stopped dead. During the night the nuts holding the governor plate had worked loose while I had been running the engine and, just at the moment I started it up again, the plate and throttle fell off leaving the engine out of control Before anything could be done to stop it a timing chain snapped and was drawn into the engine, which smashed up everything completely.

Coming at the beginning of the season, this was a calamity as I could do little without an engine. I set about searching for a suitable replacement for the Kelvin but I could not find one that could be delivered and fitted in time. In the end Tom Hedgecock, who runs the passenger boats *Nelson* and

Unity, came to the rescue and fitted a spare Morris Navigator engine which he sold to me for £60. It served my purpose for the season, although it was like asking a donkey to draw a brewer's dray. My maximum speed in still water became four knots, but when there was a headwind it dropped to nil. Still, the poor little thing ran well and tried its best.

My log of the last five years is now spinning to its close. These years have seen many alterations to my fortunes. Some of them have been good, some of them bad, but I have enjoyed myself although the risks, wear and tear to the yacht, coupled with the ever rising prices for replacing worn out gear do not give me a chance to make more than a bare living out of her in summer time. That is the reason why I purchased the general stores when the opportunity came my way. Olive manages the stores very ably while I am away and it brings in a steady income in the winter when the yacht is not earning.

Still, who knows what 1950 will hold in store? That is exactly what I like about this kind of life. One never knows what will happen next.

Probably the greatest feeling I experience is one of freedom which so many people have bartered for a doubtful security, whose sisters are scarcity, utility and taxation. This is not conducive to a feeling of well being for you can only truly feel this when you are working at something that is in keeping with your character and when you are happy at your work, irrespective of the hours you are employed or the monetary gain you get from them.

I can, without orders, proceed to sea and feel the summer rain on my face and breathe God's fresh air on the deck of the yacht. I need no permits to shake out a reef whenever I wish to get a move on, and all the National Security there is cannot help me when I am in some kind of trouble in combat with man's oldest opponents - nature and the weather. It is then that I must pull myself out of the peril by my own initiative and, inside myself, I feel a better man when I have been able to do so.

A dog chained to a kennel, is a splendid example of security. It is sure of a roof over its head because it is chained to one. Its meals are certain, but

Fresh air and no permits - a good life on Topsy

they are not rationed by its appetite or ability to catch its own food. It has the security of these two essentials but it has lost everything that once made a dog's life worthwhile. The delights of freedom and the chase have gone from it and it can now only wag its tail in gratitude to its master when he, out of the goodness of his heart, hands it its duly allotted rations on a plate.

I have secured myself by getting married and setting up a home of my own, but that chain is a man's sheet anchor and it is a natural tie accepted by all men.

I have no wish to change my uncertain profession for the certainty of employment from 8am to 6pm with a pay packet at the end of the week, and holidays with pay. My hours are as long or as short as it is expedient for me to be at the wheel or on a bridge on watch and my hours of starting are governed by the tides and weather. If you have the two great assets of health and freedom, life need never be boring and, coupled with the variety you experience, you can really live and not merely exist, cabbage fashion, as so many people seem content to do.

It is not for everyone to live or think alike, as it takes all kinds of people to make a world. But to those who do agree with me I have one message that I have learnt and that is that, supposing you are sea-minded, even the smallest boat you can afford will give you the sense of freedom of which I write, providing your voyages are governed by reason, not risk, or the tie of having to be back by 4pm because you have to change for dinner. If you cannot get back by 4pm but have to stay out until 4am, it may be most uncomfortable and not very convenient for you but it will always stand out in your memory as a minor adventure - something that can rarely come your way if you stick rigidly to set hours and habits. Believe me, you cannot become set in small ships except with the cramp.

No matter how many times one sails over the same route, it rarely appears to be the same. All the variety that the wind, weather and sea can produce alter it from time to time as do little incidents and happenings aboard the ship, while meeting with different people always lends interest.

Writing this reminds me of many interesting things that I have seen on these trips. Glorious sunsets, the shoals of fish, the migration of hundreds of wildfowl, a water spout, the antics of porpoise, lightning and the thunderstorms at sea, and a crazy shark who appeared during one of them - the memories are always there to fill the quiet, becalmed hours.

I have seen sunsets so many times but they never fail to thrill me when they are colourful and ever changing, although I have found that the old weather rhyme 'Red at night, sailors' delight' sometimes has to be taken with a pinch of salt. In 1946 when the weather appeared to me to be mild nearly all the time, I saw many beautiful sunsets off the Dutch coast.

The migration of the wildfowl was as strange a sight as I have ever seen. I described it to the writer James Wentworth Day who has since told me that he has met an old wildfowler who saw something similar many years ago.

I saw this magnificent sight when Derek and I were bringing two LCAs and three jolly boats up from Gillingham. We cut all kinds of corners to save time and it was while we were doing this that we saw the birds. We were cutting across from the South Buxey beacon across Batchelors Spit near to the bombing target that stands up like the end of a pier on the mud flats. As we approached it we could see that its shape was altered somewhat and that a broad line of dark objects stretched from it almost to the NW Knoll buoy. Our Ford V8 engines were very silent and as we came nearer we did not scare the birds, for birds they were in their thousands. The sea was absolutely oily flat calm at about high water. The time was about one o'clock in the afternoon. We steamed nearer and nearer to them and still they did not fly away and we could see them swimming around in little families like tame ducks on a pond. We stopped the boats from moving through the water when we were within stone throwing range of them and Derek and I studied them through our binoculars.

I am no wildfowler, so I cannot tell you all the different breeds that were there, but there seemed to be every assortment of bird from widgeon to duck, bar geese and geese, large and small, all paddling around. The target itself was absolutely smothered with birds. They were too far away for me to distinguish what they were. We saw this strange sight fully three weeks before wildfowl appear in any quantity in the river.

Derek and I studied them for more than a minute or two and we were surprised when they all took off as though by a pre-arranged signal. It was a wonderful sight to see that flight take the air and the whirr of wings was so loud. They flew off in an easterly direction and we watched them until they were out of sight.

I have always been puzzled why those different breeds of wildfowl were flying and resting in their hundreds together and, so far, nobody has enlightened me. Neither can I say why they were not scared of us because, as a rule, I cannot get within gun range of duck. Perhaps they were very tired. The weather was very mild at the time and many of the fishermen said that they thought it foretold another hard winter. But they were wrong for that winter was a mild one with practically no wildfowl in the river.

The water spout was seen while we were sailing off the Belgian coast on our first trip after the war. We had just passed Zeebrugge when we noticed the water spout several miles away to port near Westkepelle on the Isle of Walcheran. I had read about water spouts but this one was unlike anything I had imagined. It extended over a far greater distance than I would have believed possible and where I had expected something the colour of the sea, it was actually as black as night. It rose vertically from the sea for a while and then sagged away to leeward for a great distance to where its end again rose vertically into the clouds. The nearest thing to this sight I have seen was in a film showing a tornado in America.

We watched the water spout for a considerable time until it disappeared. It was approaching the Westkepelle lighthouse and suddenly the tall lighthouse that stands up plainly was obscured. The next moment the inky blackness was gone, leaving sheets of water falling out of the sky. I was thankful that we were no nearer to it. What it would or could have done to us I have no idea, but it did look very menacing and, at best, we would have been under a cloud burst.

A sight like that brings home to you that man and his ships are puny little things compared with what nature can produce. No matter how clever we imagine ourselves, or how important we think that we are, we really rate no greater than a grain of sand to the forces of the universe. You cannot defeat the sea or nature, but only honour and respect it. To resist a heavy sea is to court disaster as it will easily smash anything that man considers he has made strongly. It is far easier and safer to sway to the blast like a boxer riding a punch. A boat adrift will ride a sea with less chance of having gear swept away than one under power and resisting.

The sight of a shoal of fish is wonderful, too. We plough through the sea and rarely think that below us is another world, more populated than our own and with an even greater variety of life.

On a flat calm sea in brilliant sunshine one's attention is drawn to the antics of scores of seagulls over what appears to be a part of the sea on the boil and then one sees the shoal of fish, shimmering with beautiful glints of silver as they break surface. What underwater tragedy is going on there? Below and around those thousands of fish are other larger ones feeding on those that they can catch while the poor little creatures that have been forced near the surface of the water are the easy prey of the screaming gulls. Life in this world can only continue at the expense of death to some other less fortunate creatures.

Once, before the war, I was taking a steel launch into Portsmouth harbour in the dark when, as I was passing Port Blockhouse, I suddenly heard a noise something like the sound of stones being thrown at the bottom of the boat. I could not understand what it was until I saw silver glinting in the moonlight. The launch had run into hundreds of salmon bass.

One of my favourites to watch are the porpoises. What playful, curious and inquisitive creatures they are. I have stood on the bows of a mine-sweeper steaming at ten knots watching the wonderful way that they play around the bows. They weave an intricate pattern around each other and never so much as a flicker shows how they propel themselves. They will play around the craft for a long time unless you are going too slowly for them. I have been told that they will play around the bows of a destroyer travelling at speed in exactly the same way.

A thunderstorm at sea is an awe-inspiring sight, especially at night. No fireworks display could hold a candle to it. Quite a few people that I have had aboard the yacht have a natural fear of lightning and they are scared stiff by a thunderstorm at sea but I quite enjoy the heavenly display. Why they should be so scared I cannot understand for if lightning was to strike, you would know nothing about it and I cannot imagine a quicker and less painful death.

During one electrical storm we were sailing past the western entrance to Dover harbour in daylight. Everybody dashed below during the heavy downpour of rain leaving us alone at the wheel. Suddenly there was a vivid flash of forked lightning which sizzled down to the sea and a shark of some sort leapt clean out of the water vertically alongside the yacht. It writhed and twisted in the air as though it was tormented and fell back into the sea again with a heavy splash. I would estimate its length at not less than eight feet.

I shouted to the others that there was a shark alongside and they told me that I was seeing things but they came on deck, anyway, to have a look. They were fortunate, as on the next two flashes of lightning, the shark performed the same silly gymnastics and they were all able to see it for themselves.

It is interests like these that make my type of life worth living and I am looking forward to whatever the next year will bring. Who knows? Perhaps I shall have an even more interesting log to look back upon.

Previous page: An aerial view of Maldon at low tide taken in about 1960 showing the Hythe in the foreground and Fullbridge behind

BLACKWATER MEN

VOLUME TWO

By Michael Emmett

FAMILY TRADITIONS

My father's predictions about the River Blackwater becoming a playground for leisure sailors came true, of course. What he did not foresee was that his own son would be in Maldon to see those last days of commerce and fishing in the estuary. But before the end I did become one of those who made a living from the river.

My father has told how he came to Maldon and fell under its spell. My mother was born into the tight knit community of watermen he joined.

St Mary's Church stands just above The Hythe in Maldon. Known as the fisherman's church, its steeple features in so many scenic views of the river. It was into one of the cottages next to the church that my grandparents moved when they married in 1926. My grandmother had been brought up in 57 Church Street, right opposite the main gate of the church and on her wedding day the route across the road into the church was decked out with flags, as were the barges at the quay and the smacks on the Bath Wall.

My grandfather, Charles Lavender, was a bargeman from Southend. He worked for Shrimp Brand Beers of Gravesend who had a brewery on the up-river side of the ferry pier. The barrels and bottles of beer were transported by water from Kent to their Maldon warehouse which still stands on the Fullbridge wharf. A shrimp embellishing the brickwork over the main door echoes its former use.

My grandfather served in the sailing barges *Gladys, Majestic* and *Khardomah* which could all be recognised from far across the water by the words Shrimp Brand Beers painted into the topsail in large letters.

My grandmother Agnes Mary, known as Aggie, told me that the first Christmas after her marriage, the newly-weds had planned to be at home in

Opposite: St Mary's Church and the original Church Street cottages demolished in 1935

their cottage. They made the trip from Gravesend to Maldon where the barge was to be laid up for the holiday, but they had only got as far as Bradwell on Christmas Eve when it started to snow, reducing the visibility to nil. They were forced to anchor there and the anchor was not raised again until the middle of February because the river froze solid. So much for Christmas!

With the death of the managing director of Shrimp Brand, the brewery was sold to Daniels, which in turn was to be taken over by Truman. This spelt the end of the transportation of beer by sailing barge and all the barges were sold and the hands paid off. My grandfather was left unemployed, so he painted out the shed, fixed up a slab for filleting and went into the retail fish business. He bought large cod from Grimsby which he collected from Maldon East railway station to be cut and packaged for hawking round the town and outlying villages.

Gran always said he was a terrible hawker because he was too generous and kind-hearted. He was a gregarious character, always ready for a practical joke, which earned him the nickname of 'Liable' because it was said he was liable to do anything.

Relief from the less than successful fish business came when a Mr James, a wealthy London greengrocer who owned a large shop in New Quebec Street, came looking for a professional skipper for his yacht, *Manxman*. My grandfather was only too pleased to take the job. He was one of many local men, born and raised to understand the sea, winds and tides, whose knowledge and skills were recognised and appreciated by the gentlemen yachtsmen who employed them.

As he was a professional sailorman, I was always puzzled by a story my grandmother told about him losing his teeth overboard on the only occasion he ever seemed to have been seasick. Many years later, in the 1970s, I found myself working with one of his old contemporaries, 'King' Wright, and I told him the story.

He grinned and said: "T'aint sa loikely. 'E lorst 'em owt the bus winda' on the way hom' from Burnham arter a session at the Smack pub."

Another barge which belonged to Shrimp Brand Beers was *Black Eagle*. She was owned later by a well known Maldon yachtsman, Sam Poulton, who also owned the yacht, *Escape*, in which he won many cups.

Although Sam did sail the barge occasionally, she was used mainly as a houseboat, moored alongside the town's 'free hard' in Tom Hedgecock's boatyard. As well as running the boatyard and marine engineering business, Tom could be seen on summer weekends when the tides were right plying for hire on the promenade with his rowing boats and motor launches. Trips to Millbeach across the Blackwater were available in his larger boats, *Nelson* and *Unity*. In later years Sam went on these trips, too, giving a commentary on the sights to passengers. As a younger man, Sam had the distinction of riding in the very first speedway race in the country, held at the dirt track at High Beach in Epping Forest in 1928.

The *Black Eagle* sat in her berth badly one day and broke her back. She was taken up above Fullbridge where she was broken up by 'Kerly' Denny. This powerhouse of a worker did everything manually - even down to transporting huge timbers strapped to his trade bicycle. I can remember seeing him coming along the Downs Road with a couple of his many children riding on the load.

In 1935 the original cottages in which my grandparents lived in Church Street were demolished and a row of six houses was built by a local builder and property landlord, Mr Boreham. My grandparents moved into one of the new homes, number 22, in 1936 after living for a brief period in a house in Crown Lane which is now for some reason called Butt Lane.

My family's connections with Church Street started in the 1870s when my great great grandfather, Josiah Pitt, moved into number 57 and it only ended when I moved out of 22 Church Street in 1986 following my grandmother's death. This long period covers the lives of so many people who lived in those two tiny cottages. By today's standards it could be said that there was vast overcrowding with as many as nine living in one cottage at the same time but the river and the family fishing smacks along the Bath Wall gave a sense of space and freedom.

Beer bound for Maldon on a distinctive Shrimp Brand barge

THE OLD ORDER

The fishing smack, like the sailing barge, is a pretty sight on a sunny afternoon but to those who had to work them on long dark bitterly cold nights, they were merely tools and vessels of hard work. It is doubtful, though, if any of those men would have chosen a different way of making a living.

Their way of life produced characters, fiercely independent and, by modern standards, colourful, although they could not claim to be as colourful as their grandfathers who had ranged far and wide in search of a living. Nevertheless each was of note in his own right and generally each sported a nickname, some earned and some inherited from a forebear, where the origins had been lost.

The fishermen were true longshoremen because when fishing was thin they would work on the land, pea picking, fruit picking and potato lifting. Unloading timber from what they called 'steambo'ts' also supplemented the slack periods.

These motor ships used to come from the Baltic in the summertime and were laid at anchor in the river, sometimes in the Basin Reach, sometimes as far down as Stansgate. The smaller ones were taken into the canal basin at Heybridge through the locks, or on up to the Baltic Wharf to John Sadd & Sons. The Sadd lighters were towed by their own tug the *Lady Barbara* and were worked, in the main, by men on their own pay role.

The freelance fishermen worked mainly for Browns of Chelmsford, whose lighters were hulks of sailing barges that had had their gear stripped out. These lighters, once loaded, would be towed into the canal basin where the cargoes would be again transhipped into canal barges for the journey

Opposite: the Blackwater men of a previous generation - their sons and grandsons were the men my father and I knew. The group includes Johnny Willis, Jimmy and Ned Woodcraft and Walter and Charlie Stebbings

up to Chelmsford. Amongst the barges in the fleet of hulks were the *Dawn, Kitty, British Oak, British Empire, Diligent* and *Mirosa*.

The *Mirosa* had been built with the name *Ready* but Trinity House wanted the name for one of their vessels and purchased it from Francis & Gilders of Colchester who renamed the barge after Mr Francis' wife. The shipwright was to have carved MY ROSA on the stern of the boat but by mistake he carved MIROSA which still remains today.

Most of these hulks were to be re-rigged in later years and sailed as private yachts and charter vessels, once the timber carrying trade ceased with the arrival of packaged timber and mechanical handling.

Gordon Swift re-rigged and lived aboard the *Dawn*, which he then chartered for several years before selling her to the Passmore Edwards Museum. The one time owner of the Blackwater Seafood Company, Val Devall, was to re-rig and sail the *Mirosa*. He went on to re-establish oyster trading in the area - this time as a farming operation, growing on artificially spatted Japanese gigas as opposed to fishing the natural Essex natives, *Ostrea edulis*. Even Sadd's swim-headed *Montreal* has been rigged out.

The winter months, especially the hard frozen ones, meant punt gunning and nearly all Maldon fishermen were professional wildfowlers. Their punts, unlike those from other parts of the country, were open right through having no decks at all. The huge gun, eight feet or so in length, was laid in the punt with the barrel resting in a groove cut in the breast hook at the stemhead, with the butt on the thwart having a strop made fast to the thwart passed around a groove in the stock to absorb the recoil.

The man laid flat in the bottom of the punt aft of the gun with his chest resting on the gun box. This box was used to house the black powder, shot and wadding in order to keep it dry. The punt was propelled while stalking the birds, with small paddles known as hand pads. The motion was small circles, feathering on the forward stroke and pulling flat on the aft stroke. This meant that nothing had to be lifted out of the water which would have alarmed and scared the birds. The gun was aimed by directing the punt itself towards the target.

Most guns were muzzle loaders, taking a charge of black powder, although some of the 'gentlemen' gunners had breach loaders, using brass cartridges. This trade attracted gentlemen looking for sport shooting and they would hire the fishermen to take them out. The most celebrated of these was the writer and chronicler of country matters, James Wentworth-Day, who regularly went with the Claydons in the *Joseph T* and wrote extensively about their time together.

Wildfowl of all sorts were landed, especially during those dark days of the war, when a shed at the back of the Queen's Head on the Hythe was used as a collection point for the birds, under licence from the Ministry of Food. The handling agent was a Danbury man called Mr Fenwick who had a little double ended lifeboat called *Hells Bells.*

Whilst the punt gun was primarily for ducks and geese, a story I remember Cliff telling a group of us in the Queen's Head one evening put it on a higher plane.

He announced: "Oi kin tell yer all abowt me war exploits now."

Seems he had had a letter from the Ministry of Defence releasing him from the Official Secrets Act under the thirty year rule, which allowed him to talk about his part in the preparation for the invasion of England by Germany in 1940. The War Department had issued powder and shot and orders to lay in wait with the punt in the saltings ready to repel any German vessels entering the River Blackwater - shades of Dad's Army!

Cliff Stammers, an undertaker from Southminster, told his own

A steamship unloading timber at Osea Island with sailing barges to starboard and swimheaded lighters to port

story of wartime adventure on the marshes. He was in the Observer Corps and was on watch with another man out on Tillingham Marshes. They watched for enemy planes which they identified by their silhouettes, phoning through to Shoebury with the information, where the guns would sound off. As Cliff put it: "They generally couldn't hit a barn door at ten paces," but one evening they got lucky and hit one. He watched the pilot descend by parachute to a field not far from his own position. Having seen him land, Cliff and his mate decided that they had better go and get him. It did not strike either of them until later that it was probably a foolhardy thing to have done, as neither of them was armed with anything more than a pen knife.

The pilot, as it turned out, was an amicable chap and glad of the cup of tea they gave him while they tried to contact HQ on the field telephone for a vehicle to transport their prisoner. But no answer came.

"Now what? Right, Southminster police station," they decided. So they and the pilot trudged the miles up the Marsh Road only to find that it was locked up and all in darkness.

"Now what? Right, Kings Head!" The pilot was bought a drink to entertain him while they used the pub phone to try and arrange for a vehicle, which this time they managed. Returning to the bar they bought them-

selves a drink and enquired as to whether the pilot was hungry. He said he was, so they sent out for some fish and chips which he enjoyed before he was handed over as a prisoner.

The main thing that set these fishermen apart from accepted modern normalities was that they all worked until they were a great age. It was a regular sight to see a boat manned by a skipper well into his seventies, or even eighties.

I once watched with admiration a man of three score years and ten move on the mud like a man 50 years his junior. The lack of academic education was evident but their qualification from the university of nature was impeccable. They could smell a change of wind or see a weather front coming long before the forecast and generally be more accurate. Their forecasting did not need weather maps, satellites or computers. It relied on being part of the environment and having the ability to absorb signs with an ease that modern man has forgotten. How many today would recognise that the mud shines for wind and smells for rain?

Their weather lore has stood me in good stead over the years. If you wake up on a calm morning to find cobwebs hanging in the rigging, the wind will come easterly by midday.

And 'sundawgs' will always herald bad weather to follow in a day or two.

'Sundawgs' are rainbow-like flashes of colour that appear on either side of the sun as it goes down. Four days before the 1987 hurricane I saw a complete circle around the sun for the first and only time in my life. I moved my boat and warned others of bad weather on the way while the Met Office said that they had no warning of what was to come.

There was always a committee of retired and resting fishermen, bargemen and watermen sitting on the Bath Wall which overlooked the smacks laying in a long line on their port bilges on the beach which stretched from Walter Cook & Sons barge building yard at the Hythe along to the Bight. They whiled away their time watching every movement, both on and off

Above: Cliff Claydon uses the hand pads to propel his punt.

Opposite: a sadly damaged picture of Cliff in action

the water, which fuelled their discussions and added to their amusement. This gathering had the nickname of the 'tin shed parliament' as parliament sat on a plank raised on a couple of large logs at a place known as the tin shed. At the high water mark of the great flood of 1953 somebody knocked a nail into this shed showing the extreme height which the water reached that night over and above the expected predicted level.

There were many subjects talked about and debated with great fervour, regardless of whether any of the members of this parliament knew what they were talking about. This, of course, did not apply to their own territory, the water, on which they were absolute experts. At the tin shed parliament gatherings - the largest of which were Sunday mornings - the words "Thar's water over" would announce the opening of the pub, causing a mass exodus.

Malapropisms and spoonerisms were endemic. At about the time when that other parliament in London was abolishing the death penalty, a debate on the matter was being held on the Bath Wall. I quote: "Oi knows hangin' don't stop 'em murderin' but 'ats def'nately a detergent."

Unlike its London equivalent the Bath Wall had no rigid agenda and sometimes the speed at which the subject could be changed was breathtaking. Literally in the next breath after a current political discussion they might be talking about a smack that had sunk, to which might come such comment as: "Oi reckon's she's in three harves now."

The conversation would be just as impassioned and apparently important about a subject 60 years old as one that happened last week. Little was ever forgotten, even in its detail.

"Give us a fag, Pitt."

"Taint so loikely. Oi give one of you Wrights a packet of foive Woodbines when wi wus in the trenches an' Oi never did git 'um back."

They also possessed the ability to spot something different in their surroundings, however insignificant. It would be investigated and debated until it, too, became part of what was familiar - even something as small as a dark patch on the mud which had not been there yesterday.

Fishing was not just a job, it was a total way of life and this was another

Above: The scene at the Bath Wall with the tin shed parliament in session. From left they are Charlie Pitt, Meldy Wright, Dick Quilter, unidentified, Old King Wright and George Hayles

Opposite: Tin shed parliament regulars Ted Bond, Tablo Pitt and Meldy Wright

fact that set them aside. The language spoken would be described by most people as an accent, but this is only part of the truth. It was actually a complete dialect. In their offshore remote world, the fishermen had unknowingly protected Viking, Anglo-Saxon and Huguenot words and sayings. Landsmen of Essex, being infiltrated by interlopers as the fishermen called anybody from outside Maldon, had lost their speech origins long before.

The way in which fishermen spoke was known as 'Dagger Lane' after the nickname for the two streets in which most of them lived. My accent and use of words is much milder and more infiltrated than many of those men but I was told by the landlord of a pub just outside Maldon that he would buy my beer because he had not heard a true Dagger Laner for years.

The fishermen's sense of humour was also something to conjure with. Watching an aeroplane going over the son said: "Oi shunt wanna be up thar' in that."

To which came the reply from dad: "Oi shunt wanna be up thar' wi out ut."

On another occasion the son was heard to say to the father who was one of the most hard working men you could wish to meet: "Hurry up, ya lazy owd devil, Oi wanna git ashore."

On hearing this one of the other fishermen of the father's era jumped to what he thought was his defence saying: "No, no, no, Oi'm not 'aving that. Stupid 'e moight be, lazy 'e sarntently ain't."

A gentleman who has come to be known in subsequent tellings of this story as the Lord Hawbellisher, arrived on the Bath Wall resplendent in his attire, striking out in his stride and swinging a silver topped cane. Stopping to enquire the whereabouts of a barge from one of the Bath Wall octogenarians to whom he offered - far too quickly - a half-crown reward, he received the information: "Ya sees they two barges down thar', well 'ats the middle one 'o they two." Thanking him for the information, he again struck out in his stride and was seen to stop in mid-flight, cane in air, when he suddenly realised he'd been had.

The smacks existed largely because of the oyster, which gave most employment and influenced the early development of the boats, until the growth in yachting and employment for fishermen on yachts gave rise to many yacht influences showing in the smacks.

One major innovation was the introduction of the counter stern. Nearly all Maldon-built boats were bawleys. In other words they had square sterns, broad shoulders and straight stems. My great uncle Ernie had a counter built onto the bawley, *Polly* MN12, in 1922 at a cost of £50. While Walter Cook & Sons were doing this, they also removed the well-heads and blocked the wet well, a sunken part of the boat, where fish were kept alive. The bowsprit and the boom were lengthened and the topmast was removed. This would probably have made her almost unrecognisable to my great great grandfather, Josiah Pitt, who had her built in the 1880s by John Howard at a total cost of £70.

The Maldon fishermen's lives were so dictated and guided by inbred tradition and lore, that it made them conservative in the extreme, even if they did not consciously realise it. So even when engines had become universal in small craft, they still kept their sails and some never fitted engines at all. It is reputed that *Polly,* manned by Ernie and Wal, was the last commercial sailing trawler to operate in British waters.

Ernie worked until he was about 82 and his brother was eight years his junior. They were adamant that "she", as they called the *Polly*, would never have an engine and that wish is still fulfilled. She still does not have one fitted 30 years on.

For some reason the Maldoners very seldom referred to their boats by name. Instead they would say "she", "the big bo't" or simply "the smack." Many boats were named after wives, daughters, even sons or -worse - the daughters were sometimes named after the boats, giving rise to some peculiar named ladies of my grandmother's era. My family nicknamed my grandmother after the boat. She was affectionately called Pol for all her 80 years.

Ernie Pitt in typical pose on the Polly

Ernie religiously visited *Polly* on her Bath Wall berth every day when he was at home and said, very convincingly, that she talked to him. Having spent more than 70 years, five days of every week, in the same vessel, a certain amount of your spirit must be left behind and subsequent owners have vowed that they have seen him.

Longshoring was truly a family operation. My grandmother, along with her mother, were the 'marketing division'. They had a hand cart which was painted white and kitted out with scales for weighing out the fish. Chalk boards which hung on the sides of it displaying the prices. They had regular customers but they also used to hawk.

My grandmother told me that her mother could have sold snow to an Eskimo. During one lean summer when there was no work on the river, she bought a field of peas from a farmer in London Road, made the men pick them and then she hawked them round the town.

Everbody was expected to do their bit. Even my mother's girlhood pocket money came from the 'little fish money'. She sold these small fish at 4d per enamel bowl full. My mother was also expected to go pea picking to buy her winter clothes. During my grandmother's childhood there was a junk yard in Church Street and she told me that her pocket money came from the sale of worn out ground ropes, actually known as 'junk' and jam jars for which she received a penny for every ten jars.

Before the installation of engines made it possible to return to Maldon every day, regardless of wind direction, the practice was to go away on a Monday and return on the following Friday, spending the week living on the boat. Gran also told me that just after the First World War - which, incidentally, the old hands regarded as being The War, the second one being little more than a skirmish as far as they were concerned - the family had a cat named Cock. This cat made a habit of walking down to the boat with Ernie and Wal each Monday and it would watch them they were out of sight before returning home. Stranger still, it knew not only which day Friday was but also what time the tide was, for at the appropriate moment it would go down and wait on the Bath Wall for the return of the brothers in *Polly*.

Bradwell Creek was a favourite anchorage when 'working away' down the Knoll channel or in the Rays'n. One evening 'King' Wright was entering the creek, sailing the *Maud*, when he heard Ernie shout out: "Moi mate's o'board." Hearing this he rounded up, let go his anchor and rowed over to see what the situation was with thoughts of all sorts of disasters running through his mind, taking into consideration Ernie and Wal's advanced years.

But once aboard the *Polly,* Ernie greeted him with a cheery: "That't alroight though 'cos he's down below." Kingy looked through the tiny scuttle hatch to see Wal hanging out his pound and ten shilling notes to dry on a piece of yarn stretched across the hatch.

On another occasion a rather irate Ernie was found left on deck without a skiff in which to get ashore. Apparently Wal had left earlier with an arm basket full of fish to hawk around the village and had been enticed into a game of dominoes in the Green Man, forgetting all about his poor brother. Their great ages did not detract from their catching ability, for in Ernie's eightieth year they landed one of the largest lobsters ever caught on the East Coast. Their appearances in the creek at Bradwell and around the village hawking fish, have left memories that have endured over 30 years since their retirement.

MY EARLY MENTOR

I began to learn the secrets of the fishermen at the age of ten when, two weeks before Christmas 1962, I went down river with Cliff Claydon in a skiff to pick winkles for the first time. I was told to stay on the gravel while he put on his splatchers and worked off in the panways of the mud. Splatchers are nine inch square wooden plates which are strapped to the feet to prevent sinking. We returned to Maldon on the flood tide after dark and I remember being bitterly cold.

My next trip with him was in the spring and because the tide was very early we had to bike down. This meant lashing sacks onto the carrier of the bicycle and hanging the bucket on the handle bars. I met Cliff at his cottage on the Hythe at about 5.30am and we set off for Goldhanger, six miles distant. Passing down Fish Street we mounted the sea wall and rode round it another mile until we reached some gorse bushes where we hid the bicycles. We went over the sea wall into Wagers Creek to pick up winkles near the Old Sinker. Once bagged up, we carried them on our shoulders up to the bicycles, strapped them onto the carriers and the long haul home began. I did this many times but it never appealed like the trips in the skiff.

When the summer holidays came around I was once again with Cliff. This time it was Peter-netting for flounders. We rowed down the river to the Low-way by the North Doubles buoy where we laid to anchor while Cliff stood in the stern sheets of the skiff and laid the net out ready to shoot. This operation was known as 'getting the net back'.

The net was said to have gained its name from the disciple who used one on the Sea of Galilee nearly 2000 years ago. It was an anchored net, with anchors at both ends, which was shot across the tide to open it, so that

the last hour of the ebb would flow through it. Once shot, it had to be 'rugged down' which meant rowing up tide 50 to 60 yards, then going across parallel to the net hitting the ground with a pole that had an iron tip. This scared the fish out of the mud and down towards the waiting net. The process was repeated, getting closer to the net each 'over'.

Flounders would only run if the water was clear. If it was 'thick' (muddy) they would feel safe and stay still. The Peter net, then, would work in waters which were unsuitable for other gear such as trawls which required the water to have almost the consistency of soup. Hauling was always done stern to tide, picking up the leeward end first, so that the net was always pulled against the force of the elements, keeping it clear of the boat.

Once hauled, Cliff again stood in the stern sheets to overhaul the net, shaking the fish into the bottom of the skiff. We made another shot on the flood tide after which the live fish were put into the trunk. This was a small boat-shaped object with a lid on it and holes bored through, so that it floated semi-submerged in order to keep the fish inside alive.

Flounders were always counted in scores, so 42 would be two score and two, and 50 would be two score and a half. The trunk had to be towed home which was hard work owing to the fact that it had to be rowed slowly so as not to drown the inmates. Dozens of trunks could be seen moored off in the Bath Hole, where they would float even when the tide was out. When empty they were stacked against the iron railings near the tin shed.

Maldon in those days was a favourite destination for trippers in coaches or, as the locals preferred to call them, charabancs and this was the market for flounders. They were sold strung on a wire - three small ones for half a crown, whilst a 'big'un' would fetch two shillings for a single fish. There were about a dozen men in this trade and they could be seen in the afternoon sitting on the head of their skiffs, with the trunk alongside and a sign up which simply read: 'LIVE FISH FOR SALE'.

Although they were only flounders, they had adopted the name Blackwater plaice for selling purposes.

A week after my first experience Peter-netting, I was to go with Cliff again. I was told to be on the Bath Wall at 6am. When I arrived the tide was

Above: Joseph T with the Claydons at work in 1958

Opposite: Young Billy Claydon with his father on Joseph T at the Bath Wall. Cecil Wright's Roseena is in the background

Overleaf: The William with signs for live fish and oysters lies at the Bath Wall. Behind her is the Ann, Joseph T and the barge Beatrice Maud

high which seemed strange to me as when we went either winkling or netting the tide was always getting well down. There was several seabooted men launching skiffs off or working aboard the 'Big bo'ts'. Cliff arrived and spoke to another man who turned out to be his brother Alf. We all then got into a skiff that I hadn't been in before and shoved off to a smack. It was then that I realised that we were going down the river in the smack.

The smack was called *Joseph T,* named because she had been built for a man named Joseph Taylor. He only owned her for a few years as he was already an old man when it was built. She passed into the ownership of a man who had two sons called George and Frederick and she became the *George & Frederick.* She reverted to *Joseph T* MN9 on the Customs House register a little while later but 'George and Frederick' could still be clearly seen carved into the transom in the 1960s.

Brother Bill was the third Claydon but I never met him as he died before I started. Alf told me, though, that his brother Bill had worked as a paid hand for many years in the smack yacht *Betsan* for Major Paget, who also owned the large yacht *Columbine.* The Claydon brothers had bought the *Joseph T* in the late 1920s to replace their previous smack, *Black Alice,* which had broken up in high winds on Osea beach, causing the crew to have to swim for it. This gave rise to the family nickname of 'Strippy' because they had had to strip their clothes off.

It was August and the river was open, which meant that the fishermen who held licences were allowed to catch oysters from the grounds held under ancient charter by Maldon Borough Council. A closed season was enforced each year which ended in August. A ring size of $1^7/8$ inches was imposed, which meant that any oyster that would pass flat-ways through a ring of that size had to be returned to the fishery. The council provided a purpose made ring for this job.

Cliff went aft and let go both the tiller lashing and the aft mooring, while Alf set the staysail abacked, let go the inner mooring and walked the off one aft, which forced her head into the ebbing tide and around in the direction of the oyster grounds. The mainsail and jib were set up and we were sailing in company with other dredgermen although, even by this time, most of them were fully motorised. Sail dredging is generally carried out hove-to, streaming the dredges over the windward side, when the wind and tide were together. In any other direction the smack would point to windward. With the wind over the tide, the dredges would be hauled across the tide.

There were two knots used in conjunction with a 'drudge', as the fishermen called the implement. The one used to make the warp fast to the ring of the dredge was called a 'drudge hitch' and was similar to a round turn and half-hitches, except that before the single hitch was made the fall was passed through the two round turns.

Making a warp fast to the boat was by means of a back hitch around a thole pin in the capping rail of the bulwarks. The knot was half of a clove-hitch with the fall then backed over the pin. This did not jam like a clove-hitch and could be let go quickly if a dredge came tight on something on the sea bed. When a dredge came tight, the warp would be let go and a buoy which had already been attached to the end would mark the position so that it could be retrieved later. The dredges were equally spaced along the rail and hauled up by pulling the warp hand-over-hand until the ring on the top of the triangular frame was in hand. The frame was then levered on the rail which lifted the bag of 'culch' clear of the water. Then, rolling it over the rail, it was emptied onto the deck.

All kinds of things were caught - slipper limpets, old oyster shells, stones and shingle, whelks, mussels, five fingers and roses (star fish), as well as the prize oyster. Once emptied the dredge would be cast again, or 'chucked', to use the fisherman's term. It would always be chucked ring to tide to ensure that it reached the bottom the right way up. Having picked out what was saleable the residue of culch would be cast overboard using a pair of boards cut especially for the job called sheards. As oysters attach themselves to shells and limpets as spat, they have to be chipped and cleaned off. A tool known as a cul-tack, which was like a heavy blunt knife, was used for this purpose.

As sail dredging can only be performed in one direction, it meant that at the end of the oyster ground the smack had to be sailed back up wind and tide. The Claydon brothers had one piece of modern machinery, their 10hp Thorneycroft Handybilly engine, which they used to supplement the sails on the hard slog 'up hill' to the next 'drive'.

Arthur and Charlie Pitt oyster dredging

Low water was always breaktime, sometimes laying to the dredges if there was not too much wind. If there was, then the smack would be anchored up to windward.

No kettle was used when the fishermen made tea. The teapot had the tea and the water put into it and was placed on the coal stove to boil. The old tea leaves were only emptied out when there was not enough room for three cups of water to be put in it. When ready, it was poured into mugs with Nestles milk and heaps of sugar. It took on the appearance of dark treacle and tasted out of this world.

After changing the gear from one side to the other ready for flood tide, the work was carried on until half flood, when the gear was coiled up and the decks washed down while taking the tide up to Maldon.

My next trip out with Cliff was dredging again, but instead of working the whole tide we left off early and made for West Mersea. The Claydons sold oysters to, amongst other buyers, Bentleys of Piccadilly, who had oyster laying at Mersea. We were to meet Chick, Bentleys' man, to whom we were to 'put out' our week's catch.

Oysters were bought and sold either by the count - one hundred at a time - or by an ancient volumetric measure know as the Wash. The Wash measure was a shallow barrel containing 22 quarts and 1 pint and was a fraction of a Winchester Bushel. Large oysters were bought by the count and were added up by holding three in one hand and two in the other, counting this as one. So when 20 was reached you had one hundred. A spare oyster would be set aside to designate each hundred. At the end of the count the spare oysters would be counted and this would give you how many hundreds there were.

By the time school allowed me another holiday to go down river again, the winkling season had begun. The year was rounded off for me on Boxing Day, when I helped pull the smack on as close to the Campshed as we could get her, so that she would avoid the ice as much as possible. It was the start of that bitter winter of 1963, when the river froze solid for some miles down and it was reported that the sea froze at Whitstable.

LIVING FROM THE RIVER

Years ago the oyster trade at Maldon largely depended on the catching of brood and immature oysters, known as half-ware, from the Several and Free fisheries. The Free were grounds around our coast not covered by charters that followed Magna Carta. They therefore belonged to the Crown and the freemen of England were allowed to work them. The Several fisheries were grounds held by councils, companies and sometimes individuals under orders made by Parliament with permission from the Crown Estate Commissioners. These grounds required licences from the appropriate governing body. In Maldon's case the fishery was held under ancient Royal Charter originally granted in 1171 and endorsed by subsequent monarchs for many centuries. They issued licences which, when I first started, were known as the 'five bob licence'.

The Maldon boats would catch immature oysters which would then be sold to merchants who had oyster layings which needed re-seeding. The main market was at West Mersea where the creeks of the Quarters, such as Thorn Fleet and Buzzan were marked off by withies into plots each owned by different merchants. A withie was a sapling stripped almost to the top and stuck into the mud at a pre-determined position. All laying and dredging operations could then be conducted using these marks.

The boundary marks were three 'withies in transit' known as 'metes'. In other words when the three saplings appear in a line from the smack, that is the boundary line. The moving of immature oysters to these beds was necessary to fatten the meat content. Land drainage of fresh water which reduced the salinity of the water was regarded as helpful to the fattening

process, as long as it did not come in flood proportions. The grounds were harrowed and bottomed with shell after all pests and debris had been removed.

The oyster is an hermaphrodite, choosing its sex by the conditions prevailing at the time. They reproduce by releasing a milky-like substance from both male and female which mixes in the water. They are said then to have 'thrown a spat'. It floats for some days in this form, with the microscopic individuals swimming within the spawn-like substance. This is enough for it to maintain its position on the tide so that it will return to its parent stock at the time it sinks to the bottom and attaches itself to a convenient shell or stone. This will happen unless adverse weather or tides occur in which case the spat will be spread far and wide or, indeed, destroyed. At this stage it resembles a piece of tallow about as big as the end of a Woodbine cigarette.

From this it passes through the brood stage, when it is about the size of an old florin, on to the half-ware stage which is one season off being marketable in the lower grades.

The oyster is now about four years old and is prime for removal from the spatting grounds to be relaid on the fattening beds. The new seedlings may only require one season to fatten up or sometimes as many as three to reach the large grades. When they reach maturity they are called ware and are graded from number 4 - the smallest - to number 1, with the very large oysters being known as Royals.

Sorting oysters on deck

During the season, which covers the months which have an 'R' in them - September to April - the ware would be dredged and stored in pits. These ponds were especially dug in the saltings where the water revitalized itself fortnightly during the spring tides. This enabled oysters to be graded and held in readiness for when orders were received. Since the 1930s a government control order has meant that oysters have had to undergo purification. This involves placing the oysters in tanks where the water is passed through an ultraviolet light killing the bacteria. The oyster, as a filter feeder, then

Opposite: the author preparing winkles for market in 1968

cleanses itself in the cleaned water. Certificates of purification are issued by the local authority who take samples weekly and test for E-coli levels - a bacteria from the gut of man. In addition, if oysters are to be sold on Billingsgate market a further sample has to be tested by the Worshipful Company of Fishmongers who issue their own certificate.

Where an oyster spats or where it is laid, is where it lives its immobile life. Being a filter feeder, it must be the most inoffensive animal in God's creation, yet it has been the cause of much argument and violence. Treated like gold at times, it has created an atmosphere in which men would fight over rights, boundaries and - worse - greed. In fact, the last case heard in the British courts under the ancient piracy acts was heard at Witham Magistrates Court in April 1894, against a group of Tollesbury fishermen.

They had observed some Burnham boats removing culch from the Shawl, near the Bench Head off Brightlingsea, recognised at that time as being the most important free fishery in Europe. This created a lot of ill feeling because the removal of culch would destroy the fishery just as removing the top soil from farmland would result in its destruction.

After some weeks the Tollesbury men felt so strongly about the depletion of the fishery that they took the law into their own hands. On the day in question, four Burnhamites were dredging culch, which they would relay in the Crouch, when three Tollesbury smacks bore down on them with apparently only two or three in the crew. Once alongside, a dozen or more Tollesbury men who had been concealed in the holds came out armed with sticks and shovels. They boarded the smacks *Emmeline, Alma* and *Wonder,* threatened the crew and returned the cargo of culch to the bed of the river. Giving chase to a fourth boat, *Rose,* they found one of her crew armed with a 12-bore shotgun which he solemnly swore he would discharge at anybody who tried to board his vessel and so *Rose* was allowed to escape. The crews of the other three smacks were allowed to go after a few hours and returned to Burnham.

Reprisals were discussed in the heat of the moment but sense prevailed and advice was taken from solicitors to the Admiralty who directed that it should be treated as a case of piracy. The magistrates court was filled with over 300 fishermen from Tollesbury and Mersea which shows the height of the emotive feeling and the solidarity of the men from those villages. Five of the defendants were committed for trial at the Chelmsford Assizes in June where the sensible judge decided and directed that the charge of piracy was far too strong for a case which really should have gained its redress by civil means. The fishermen said in their defence that they were trying to protect the fishery for the common good. To which the judge directed the jury to consider that no man should be found guilty of trying to protect property belonging to the sovereign. The jury took only a short time to find all the defendants not guilty - a verdict which caused much jubilation.

The oyster has a long list of predators including; crabs and boring whelks (tingles), roses and five fingers (starfish), slipper limpets and, not least, the West End connoisseur who eats them with gin and gingerbread.

The hand hauled oyster dredge has not changed in its design for 2000 years. The Roman occupying forces at Colchester would certainly have recognised the dredge shown in the appendix on page iii as the implement which supplied them with one of their favourite seafoods.

There are records showing that oysters were sent to Rome from Colchester. One emperor is said to have believed that the only good thing about Britain was its oysters. Evidence of the Romans presence in the river sat for many years on my Uncle Tablo's window sill in the form of large shells of Mediterranean origin which he had dredged out of the silt.

To work a hand dredge, it is given sufficient warp to allow the heel to touch the ground so that the cover between the upper bar and the scythe designates the cut. The dredged material goes over the scythe and into the bag behind. This is made up of the ring hide, similar to a net but made of wire rings on the bottom which takes the chaff, and ordinary trawl netting on the top.

Originally the net and the ring hide would have been laced together with leather, but in recent years strips of rubber cut from car inner tubes have been used. A stick on the back of the bag holds the net wide and makes a handle for emptying the net. It also keeps the net clear of the frame while the dredge is cast, or 'chucked'. In the past, the making of ring hides was a job for the winter evenings. Made from stout wire, they were formed into rings of about two inches in diameter which were completed with interlocking enclosed eyes with the aid of a pair of round nosed pliers. Each ring was joined to the next by a curl of wire resembling a spring.

When oysters or, for that matter, winkles lay in deep narrow creeks, making normal dredging impossible, they would be tow hauled. This operation involved putting a hand dredge and warp in a skiff and dropping her bow anchor at the up-tide limit of the ground meant to be worked. Her

The Harriet Blanche in Thorn Fleet. In the background is the Tollesbury and West Mersea Oyster Company's oyster packing station

Overleaf: Michael Emmett and King Wright culling winkles on the Bath Wall in 1974. Photograph by Den Phillips

painter, with an extra warp attached, would then be paid out until the skiff had drifted some way downstream, then the dredge was chucked over the stern and the bow warp hauled upon, pulling along the skiff and the dredge until the anchor was almost reached. The dredge was hauled and emptied while the skiff was allowed to drift back downstream ready for the next tow.

Dredging for oysters would continue until the first frosts of winter made the ground hard and stopped the dredges from cutting into the culch properly. The old hands referred to this as 'the ground being shut.' This, coupled with the shorter days led most fishermen to go winkling.

The lowly winkle played a great part in the yearly cycle of some of the fishermen. Starting in October and finishing in April, the winkling season represented more or less half the working year. During this time the man would be bent double for up to six hours a day, straightening only to load the skiff or bicycle for the long haul home which could be six or seven miles on the road or an equally hard row on the water. Winkles were gathered in various ways - all of them by hand. They lay on the mud in small clusters or gathered around the large stones or rocks. One strange thing about winkling was that you could always see more winkles on the flood tide, especially as the water was running over them. It is my belief that they live not only on the surface, but burrow and live beneath it, too. When they feel the tide swelling up through the ground they come out to meet the oncoming water which brought food in their direction.

A bucket which had a ridged handle, usually made from a supple stick cut from the hedgerow was used to collect the winkles in. Another container, called a tindle, was sometimes used, too. It had a similar shape to a flower seller's basket and was made with a wire mesh covering which enabled the catch to be washed. Winkles could also be washed in the bucket because it had holes drilled in the sides which allowed the water to drain through. A further aid to washing was the purse net, or 'puss net', which was made of small mesh fish netting and would hold about a peck - two gallons.

Winkles would gather together in the creeks and drains - 'cricks and dreens' - following the early frosts of the year and form quite large piles around snap weed in the spring. A lard net which resembled a butterfly net was used when winkles laid this dense. It would be held in one hand and placed in front of the pile while the winkles were flicked into the bag with the other hand. Another way was to sweep - 'dygle' - the winkles out of the waters of the creeks, using the lard net like a dredge on a handle. Great quantities could be gathered by this method if you were lucky enough to find them in large groups. I once took 27 bushels out of Coopers Creek on the south shore of the Blackwater in three low waters.

Over at Stumble which is to the north of Osea Island, there is an obstacle called The Hard. This is the causeway that joins the island to the mainland at Decoy Point. It meanders across the mud, bisecting the creek which, to the north, is called Stumble Dreen and to the south Ford Crick.

The barrier could only be crossed by skiff at about half tide which made many tides impossible to work in one day. One way to get around this problem was to bike down and leave the bagged up winkles on a buoy line, to be picked up on the high water with the smack. It was just possible under motor to leave Maldon as soon as she was afloat - 'fleet' - get over the hard, pick up the bags and return in time to moor before the tide ebbed away. Another way was to row down, saving water over the hard on the ebb and leave the skiff anchored. Taking a bicycle in the skiff you could return home each evening by road after gathering the winkles. The skiff would then be rowed home with its cargo and the bicycle later in the week.

The only other way was to circumnavigate the island, but this was a journey of nearly three times the distance. When the wind was favourable a small lug sail or, more likely, a leg-o-mutton sail would be set to assist the rowing.

The smack's decks loaded with winkles picked from the Stumble, on the north side of Osea Island

Once home, the work started again. The winkles which, in the main, were encrusted with barnacles were sacked up and trodden on. This grinding and rolling action rubbed the barnacles off. This done, they were washed in a basket, sieved through a half inch mesh and tipped out onto a sack. Many stones and shells would have been collected while picking and these had to be removed before the winkles were measured into bushel sacks (1 bushel = 4 pecks = 8 gallons). For all this labour the payment when I first started was 36 shillings a bushel.

The amount of winkles gathered at Maldon at one time can be illustrated by the fact that, in addition to the private buyers such as small shops who took regular supplies, a railway cart from Maldon East Station paid two visits every week during the season to take away a full load of sacks which had been stitched and had consignment notes and labels attached. These were destined for Billingsgate, Norwich and markets in the Midlands from where they found their way back to the seaside again, to places such as Blackpool and Southend, as well as into the public houses and street-markets of the East End of London.

The closed season for shellfish, as laid down by the borough council fishermen's licence, was from 15th June to 31st July each year. The licence stipulated that no rights were to be exercised except the right to catch 'floating fish with hook and line, and soles, flounders, mullet, skate, thornback and garfish by net.'

The water at this time of year always went 'as clear as gin' and much weed and jellyfish floated up and down on the tide, which made trawling ineffective. At night the water was said to be 'on fire'. This was caused by microscopic organisms emitting phosphorescence which will illuminate fishing gear almost as if it were plugged into mains electricity. This was the time when some of the men went onto the land for work or unloaded the 'steambo'ts'. Others practised network, such as Peter-netting, eel and mullet dragging, grubbing and babbing, which was not so badly affected by these problems.

Grubbing and babbing must be among the most simple and ancient forms of fishing. Grubbing was the catching of flounders by hand. The man would stir the mud upstream so as to thicken the colour of the water then, starting downstream, he would gradually work his way up against the flow of the tide feeling the bottom until a flounder was located. Holding it down with his thumbs, he would slide his fingers under the body and it then lift the fish into a purse net hanging from his belt.

Eels were caught by babbing. This rod and line operation involved no hooks but the bait of lug or garden worms was threaded longways onto about 18 inches of worsted with a special long needle. This was then curled twice and tied onto a line along with a lead weight. A short stick acted as the rod and the line was simply rolled around the end of the stick so there was no need for a reel.

The fisherman would sit in a low sided punt, hanging the line over the side until the weight touched the ground. He would then raise it slightly and the eel, passing on up the river on the early flood, would bite on the worms entangling his teeth on the worsted. The fisherman, feeling a tug on the line, would lift it into the punt and knock the eel off into the bottom.

A day's babbing might start as far down as the shoals at Millbeach, working the first of the flood up through the Basin Flat, Smack Hole, the Bath Hole, on up to the Bridge Hole and Beeleigh. Constant moves of anchorage in this way meant that the depth of water could be kept to a minimum.

By the time I started on the water these methods were already only used for entertainment and sport, except for one old hand named Jack 'Belty' Sextan, who still made his living from grubbing, babbing and Peter-netting. This agile, slight octogenarian rowed his punt for miles practising his trades - a feat in itself as the punt resembled a packing case or a coffin more than it did a boat.

Maldon as a trawling station had been dying since the Second World War, mainly because of growing pollution coming down the rivers from inland towns and the dumping of high explosives in the estuary after the war. By the end of the 1950s most of the fishermen were concentrating on the dredging of oysters and gathering winkles.

King Wright tried to tell me: "All you need is a drudge iron and pail." But did I listen?

The major factor in the decline of trawling was that the commercial fishing grounds were getting further and further to seaward and Maldon was as far inland as the long Blackwater estuary could put her, making passage times uneconomical. The exception to this, for a while, was shrimping which was carried out with a small mesh beam trawl.

Ged and Ken Wright with a good day's catch on the Harriet Blanche

Ernie's brother, Tablo, along with his sons, Arthur, Reg and Charlie, worked the *Tinymite* MN37 which had been built by Shuttlewoods of Paglesham and had originally been powered by a steam engine. During their ownership she was fitted with a three cylinder Lister diesel engine. Her name was something of an anomaly as she was actually the largest vessel to be worked from Maldon at that time. The catch of shrimps had to be cooked on board and then laid out in trays to dry, so *Tinymite's* vast expanse of deck was invaluable. She had been purchased just after the war to replace their two smaller smacks, *Grace Darling* MN7 and *Thistle* MN243. Tablo had sold them because of his advancing years and his wish to work collectively on one boat.

At the age of 69, Tablo found himself catching and transporting freshwater fish for the Chelmer and Blackwater Navigation. The lock gates at Heybridge had to be renewed and the fish moved further up the river so they would not die with the influx of salt water into the fresh water.

Another shrimper was Ernie's nephew Tom who, with his son, Chris, and sometimes Jack Meadows, worked the Leigh-built bawley *Letitia* MN19. This vessel had been built for the Osbourne family in 1939 and had gone to Dunkirk as one of the "little ships" to fetch back members of the Expeditionary Force.

The word smack simply means fishing boat and so the vessels took on many guises. They were constantly evolving to suit changes of usage and in later days they were affected by yachting fashion. There were boats like the *Boadicea* CK213 which had originally been built in Maldon in 1808 as a clinker built vessel and was then replanked and lengthened as a carvel bawley sometime later that century. Boats were sometimes lengthened in the centre and counters added. The practice of lengthening was quite common at Brightlingsea where redundant oyster smacks were expanded to gain hold space for spratting in the stowboat trade. Brightlingsea was at one time the largest exporter of sprats to Eastern European countries and there were vast yards in the village where they were pickled and barrelled.

Smacks were not always built in what we accept as recognised boatyards because, before the intervention of the crippling planning powers enjoyed by local authorities, any spare piece of land would be used for boat building. The tiny piece of ground at the bottom of St Mary's Lane, the yard of the Queen's Head and even back gardens were used. The smack *Ant* MN60 was built in such a garden at Brightlingsea for Joss Frances. She was the most odd shape with what can only be termed as an upside down bulbous bow, having a dramatically cut away forefoot and a tumblehome only equalled by a Yorkshire cobble. The story goes that she was built like that so that when she was to be turned around and brought out of the garden for launching, her forward end would swing over the brick garden wall which their land-

Arthur and Charlie Pitt shrimp trawling

Opposite: Tablo Pitt with Thistle

lord would not allow them to demolish. When I first started on the water Joss's son, Dick, was the fishery officer for the Kent and Essex Sea Fisheries Committee. For all the *Ant's* peculiarities of appearance, she was said to be a handy little boat for oystering in the narrow creeks because she would 'tarn on a tanner.'

Nets were sometimes completely handmade and the method used by Maldon fishermen was called back hitching. This differed from braiding, the method used by factory girls while making trawls. Apart from the difference in hand action, the finished net had all the sheetbend knots on the same side in every row while braided nets had the knots laid alternately. The art of net making was taught to me by my great uncle Wal when he was in his 90th year and we made many yards of Peter net together.

Once the 'lint', as the netting was called, had been made, it had to be hung in the fishing lines. These would be stretched and then fixed at about chest height along the garden, where the netting could be joined to them. Netting was always hung with a certain amount of slack so that it achieved flow and put the strain onto the ropes. Different nets required differing amounts of slack. Peter nets were always 'put in by the thirds'. Two mesh lengths were measured along the line, but three were hung in that space.

But making nets was already a dying craft and more often the lint would be bought from suppliers of machine-made netting such as J W Stuart of Mussleburgh in Scotland, who sold cotton netting and yarns for Peter nets and drags. Trawls usually came from Bridport-Gundry or the Coal, Salt and Tanning Company at Lowestoft. Lines could be purchased in Maldon from the sailmakers, Arthur G Taylor and Son. I remember buying some bass dredge warps from Fred Taylor, who measured them out by the stretch of his arms - equal to one fathom. Cotton netting had to be constantly dried to prevent it rotting and this was done by hanging the net by the lines which were threaded onto a pole and then hove up the mast. Drags and trawls were always dressed with a solution of Catechu or bark which gave them a tanned appearance. The Peter nets were always left white, though, or perhaps just trodden into the mud to discolour them.

Mending a broken net was a different operation to making new netting and my tutors in this job were King and Lucka. It was a bit like doing a jigsaw puzzle but first you had to cut away to enable the new stitching to match in. The rule was to start off from a half mesh and to be able to recognise when to pick up the unbroken meshes in order to complete. Sometimes what appeared to be a huge hole could amount to just a few broken meshes. 'Halvers' and 'claws' which were nothing more than the odd mesh missing were difficult to spot but were probably more crucial than a big hole, especially in an eel net. Eels have a way of finding an escape route when there does not appear to be one.

A CAREER IN FISHING

The purchase of my first little smack came in 1968 when I was 16. Alf Claydon had sold his big smack, *Joseph T*, in 1964 and bought the 27-footer *Happy Days* MN6 for use in his retirement. Having decided that he could no longer look after her, he sold her to me - but not all at once. The deal was struck, the paperwork filled in and exchanged through the Customs House. Although she was only a tiny vessel of three tons gross, she was registered not only under Part IV of the Merchant Shipping Act, 1894, as MN6 but also under Part 1 with the official number 164131.

The bill of sale, signed over a red seal, transferred 'sixty four sixty fourths shares in the ship, her boats, guns, ammunition, small arms and appurtenances', almost as if she was a first ship of the line. Her year of building was unknown but must have been sometime early in the last century.

She was a complete boat inside another. Originally she had been clinker built and transom sterned, with ropeways for rowing. At some time, probably about 1890, the construction had been overlaid with carvel planking and a counter stern had been added along with an iron ballast keel. She was said to have been one of the Colchester Oyster Fishery protection vessels. These vessels patrolled the oyster grounds of the River Colne both night and day, manned by one uniformed constable in each boat.

Cliff told me that he had been warned by one of these boats when he was working down along Mersea shore in the 1920s, because he had been dredging too close to the metes which are marked on that fishery by white fishery buoys.

At the outbreak of the Second World War she was owned by Harold

Blind, who used her as a yacht. It is reputed that he was a blackshirt and that he had been caught sailing off across the North Sea from where he had been returned by the Royal Navy. His tombstone in Maldon cemetery has an engraving of the boat on it, which only goes to show how much it meant to him.

When I say that Alf did not sell the boat to me all at once, I mean that I received the hull with the engine in it first of all but then I was gradually given pieces of gear and equipment week by week, visit by visit, seemingly in return for helping Alf in some way - either by mending his skiff, making net or even digging his allotment. We became great friends and I spent a lot of my weekends and spare time at his bungalow or down the river with him. It came as a great shock when I learnt one day that he had died. It was the end of an era.

Wooden boats, flax mainsails and gaff rig were among the victims of the disease and fever that swept through the whole of life in the 1960s - that widespread desire to destroy all old structures, institutions and values and replace them with all things modern.

Thankfully, there were a few that felt that to have a present and a future of worth, it must be built on a past. One of these was John Bray who, along with John Scarlet, founded the Old Gaffers Association. John Bray worked for J D Potters of the Minories in London as an Admiralty chart agent and was a highly intelligent, true English eccentric. He lived on an old Falmouth quay punt called *Nell*, a yacht of some 16 tons which he had bought for £208. The £8, he told me, were for the solicitor's fees. Although we did sail together in her, we spent more time discussing mathematics over a pint or two in the Queen's Head. My knowledge in that subject and what little I know of the English language, as spoken today that is, is due entirely to him, as are my drinking habits.

From the first days of the association, when it was honestly believed that the Old Gaffers Race was to be the swan song of a type of boat and rig that was to shortly disappear, until the days when he saw almost 100 entries for the race which by this time had been given a permanent base for the day at the Stone Yacht Club, John Scarlet was the Old Gaffer's secretary.

Happy Days on the day Michael Emmett bought her in 1968

*Opposite:
Alf Claydon*

I sailed with John Bray in *Nell* during one of the first races which, in those days, ended in Brightlingsea with the prize giving at the Yachtsman pub. In later years I entered *Happy Days* for the race which started off at the Stone and went seaward to the Wallet Spitway buoy, across the Priory Spit buoy and then home for the prizegiving in the Stone Yacht Club.

We did not win anything but a large pilot cutter called *Theodora* which was run at that time by the Ocean Youth Club had done rather well. Cliff, who had been invited to sail as mainsheet man, decided to celebrate. After having one, or perhaps two, too many he was carried home and put to bed. I went to see him the following morning and found him sitting on his back doorstep with his head in his hands.

He gazed slowly up at me and moaned: "Oi ain't comin' owt wi' you lot no more."

And as far as I can recollection he never did, except for the odd Guinness and game of cribbage in the Queens.

My day job at this time was as an apprentice shipwright at Dan, Webb and Feesey where the whole labour force were either smacksmen or sons of smacksmen. Roy Pitt, one of the shipwrights, had joined the firm during the bad winter of 1947 but before then he had been fishing with his father and brother 'Alfa', in the little *Skylark* MN4, which had originally been built as a pleasure boat carrying trippers at the seaside - hence her name. Peter Wright, another shipwright, was the son of Sam 'Emma' Wright, who owned the *Harriet Blanche* MN42. His crew were nicknamed the Trilby Gang because of their preference for that particular type of head gear.

The painters and watermen were Sam's brother, Sid 'Tubby' and his son, Ged. Tubby crewed a yacht called *Nutcracker* during regattas and races for a Maldon businessmen called Jim Gozzet who owned a coachworks and garage in the town.

After qualifying, I joined Norton Marine at Heybridge Basin. The foreman shipwright, Jim Barbrook, was a native Tollesbury man whose father had owned smacks during their heyday. Jim told me that the first Tollesbury smack to have an engine fitted was the *Rosenna*. When she had a four horse power Kelvin installed, his father along with many others went to view this new development. On his return he declared that he was selling the smacks because in his opinion: "That machine will shake the boats apart and ruin the fishery."

The Tollesbury oyster grounds were held by a type of company which had been granted a Several Order by Parliament in the 1870s, restricting the usage only to the fishermen of Tollesbury, West Mersea, St Lawrence and Bradwell. In order to become a full member of the dredgerman's company the boys of those villages had to serve an apprenticeship.

One morning breaktime at Norton's a discussion started as to who was a *bona fide* fisherman. Jim reckoned he was the only genuine fisherman because he could still produce his indenture paper. He also told me that he spent the summers before the war serving in yachts, mainly of the steam variety.

While we were rebuilding a Medway conservancy tug called the *Ferret* which had been hauled out at Cardinals Boatyard in Maylandsea under a dispensation agreement, Jim re-made the acquaintance of a man who had also served in the same steam yacht. It amazed me how quickly they recognised each other considering it had been 35 years since their previous meeting.

So to the professional fisherman, I was just a 'weekender' selling my own fish on the Bath Wall while Cliff sold the winkles I gathered to a fishmonger called Mr Bragg with whom he had been dealing since before the war. By this time Cliff was only going down the river occasionally to supplement his pension and his last trip was to pick winkles at Clarks Beacon.

This happy situation was to alter rather rapidly with the sudden collapse of Nortons which left me looking for work just before Christmas. As nothing was forthcoming in the boatyard trade, I went winkling every day to earn my wages with the intention of looking for shore work after the festivities. As it turned out I never did and my professional fishing career had begun.

Just before the shipways went into liquidation, I had sold the little three ton *Happy Days* and bought the 15 ton *Mollie* CK142, which was re-registered MN95, from a West Mersea fisherman called Douglas Stoker.

Happy Days under sail

She was a very heavily built Harwich bawley powered by a 120hp Perkins diesel with a belt driven winch to the foreside of the wheelhouse. Jim had come with me to view the vessel before I bought it and was of the opinion that she was generally in a serviceable condition. He said that, like all old boats, she needed some work but that none of it was beyond repair. He did have some reservation about her keel because it was in the mud and out of sight. But on his advice I felt happy to proceed. She was slipped at Dan, Webb and Feesey for initial fitting out. While we watched her being hauled clear of the water, or 'seuwed' as the local term has it, Peter Wright remarked: "Where's the keel?"

"What keel?" I replied.

Overleaf: The Mollie leaves Maldon for a night's drifting

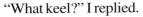

"Precisely," he answered.

Over the next couple of weeks a massive lump of elm was located and purchased, along with bolts, nearly two feet in length, and some cow hair and coal tar which was to be used as bedding material.

'Clodblocks' were 'dogged together' forming the shape of the turn of the bilges of the bottom. She was suspended on these with her keel - or at least the place where it should have been - clear of the cradle to allow free entry and working space. The elm bulk was marked out to the shape of the boat. She had taken on a shape over the years that was far from straight. It was then adzed to the scribed marks, hauled under her, the bedding liberally applied and then she was bolted up.

Despite the problems buying the boat was a good decision because, in the long run, I was very pleased with her.

Although she had originally been built as a sailing vessel, she had not carried sails for many years. My intention was to rig her for sailing and fish part-time, but when fate dealt me a new hand with the closure of Nortons, it meant that *Mollie* had to be treated as a purely commercial venture and she remained a motor vessel during my ownership. She has now been re-rigged by Roger Hardy and attends regattas and races as a yacht. He also owns the *Victory* which was built for the Royal Whitstable Oyster Company to replace their earlier vessel the *Victorious*.

My cousin, Tony, also found himself seeking work after Christmas and came as mate with me. He had a motor car which we used to travel as far as Osea Hard, from where we would walk sometimes up to two miles on the mud, depending upon where we had decided to go winkling. We always bagged them up and left them on buoy lines to be collected with the *Mollie* on a high water, using her derrick and whipping drum to lift them out of the water. There were plenty of winkles there at that time and, with two of us picking, large amounts soon accumulated. Sometimes they half filled the bawley's decks.

One day when we were picking, we noticed a lot of motor fishing vessels in the lower part of the river, an area known as Pont which is the old name for the River Blackwater. In fact, above Braintree today it is still known as the Pant.

Being curious we took the car back through Maldon to Steeple Stone. On arriving, we found many boats, some big enough to call little ships, lorries and so many fish boxes that the place had the appearance of one of the major trawling stations. Herrings had drawn them all there and a short discussion in the car propelled us into the drifting business.

I bought ten 45 feet deep cotton drift nets from Paul Willament who ran the Longshore Supply Company at Gorlestone, near Yarmouth. These second-hand nets had come off Scottish steam drifters that had worked the North

Sea. We were able to cut the nets in half, making two out of every one which still left more than enough depth for the Blackwater and Colne estuaries. Even though they had been cut down, they sometimes 'snagged on old England' as the old hands called the bottom.

Our first trip produced 210 stones of fish which the haulier and fish merchant, Richard Hayward of West Mersea, took to Colby's at Lowestoft market where they made £5 for each seven stone box. It was a remarkable increase in earnings considering we had been winkling for £25 per week each.

Sometimes when fish were caught on a Saturday night it meant that the boat would be alongside Maldon Quay on Sunday morning with the catch on deck.

One particular Sunday I had phoned the haulier to come and pick-up the fish and got back to the boat where I found the crew selling dozens and half dozens of herrings at a time to people on the quay. They had almost run out of newspaper to wrap the fish in so I went up the hill to where I lived to fetch some more.

Once home, my grandmother asked me how we had got on the night before and I not only told her about the catch but also about the people on the quay. She found as much paper as she could and I went back to the boat to find an enormous crowd had gathered. I obviously had not got anywhere near enough paper, so up the hill I went again. This time my grandmother stopped what she was doing, told me to go back to the boat and said she would go around all the cottages in Church Street and North Street to collect newspaper.

Mollie at Maldon Quay with herrings ready to discharge

She was soon down at the quay where she set-up temporary work surfaces made out of fish boxes, organised queues and directed the selling operation with the fervour of a Billingsgate trader. By the end of the morning we had sold 170 stones of fish. The only thing left to do was cancel the lorry and go to the pub!

My cousin, who did not have the spirit of a fisherman, found himself a job ashore and got married. I then had a succession of young mates, including Jamie Scott, who was the son of a fishermen who had come to live in Maldon on a converted Dutch barge. He was the best mate I had at that time and I was saddened to hear that he had been tragically killed some years later on a trawler working in the Western Approaches.

On one occasion we had shot 20 net which we left to drift while we motored back to Steeple Stone to land some winkles. The Leigh shellfish merchant Bob Rawling, who was a relative of the Osbourne family who had had the *Latitia* built, was to meet us there and collect them with his van. All went well until on the return journey to find the gear we ran out of diesel. Luckily I had a leg-o-mutton sail and foresail for the *Mollie*, so we were able to sail onto the end of the nets, pick up the 'dahn buoy' and haul them. When we reached them we found Gordon Swift in *Early Bird* MN87 hauling his gear. Gordon used to catch herrings in the winter months to supplement his income whilst his charter barge *Dawn* was laid up. Once he had got his nets on board he came over to see what was wrong and offered to tow us to Maldon which we gladly accepted as the wind was dead westerly.

A herring net hangs like a curtain in the water and is allowed to drift with the tide, the fish 'gilling' into the mesh. The gear would be shot at about half ebb, if working in the river, to be stood by until it had drifted down to low water and then back up with the flood. It was hauled in by hand over whichever side suited the wind direction. Once on board, the net would be pulled over a pole suspended from the top of the wheelhouse reaching forward to be lashed to the mast, parallel to the deck. Shaking the net as it was pulled over, the fish would drop to the deck leaving just a few that had to be picked out by releasing their gills from the mesh.

Although it was mainly herring in the catch sometimes whiting, mackerel, gurnards, smelts, garfish and even the odd cod or mullet were taken. In the early spring the herring spawned on the Eagle Bank between Brightlingsea and Clacton where large quantities were taken in a very short space of time. Working on the high water, the net would sometimes have to be hauled almost as soon as it was shot because it would be sinking with the weight of fish. Hauls of many tons were common.

Overfishing led to the downfall of this trade. A total ban at one time put many boats out of business, then small quotas and restricted seasons made it uneconomic for those left, even after the Ministry of Agriculture, Fisheries and Food lifted the ban.

It was time for me to make another change of direction by selling the *Mollie* and buying a 22-ton sidewinder trawler from Grimsby called the

Better Hope GY272. I thought then that trawling was the answer. Trawled fish such as Dover sole, skate (roker) and plaice fetch a much higher price than herrings, but the nett profits and therefore wages are not so good because of higher running costs, the main offender being fuel. So after one season cutting even, she was laid up for sale and I wished I had listened to my mentor, Kingy, who had warned me to stay with the dredge.

The *Better Hope* was a very un-lucky boat for me because although she was a well found vessel she had a tendency to go in for small break-downs at the most crucial moments.

On one occasion I was trawling on the Bench Head. It was evening with the visibility closing in and the wind strengthening from the south, when the gearbox seized and stopped her 100 hp Gardner diesel engine. I took her out of gear and tried the starter. The engine went first time but when the gear lever was pushed for-ward it stalled again. We decided that the best thing to do was to haul the fishing gear and drop the anchor which we did without much trouble.

The next problem was then to work out our position. I checked the depth of water and worked out how long it was until low water which led me to believe that while we had been getting the gear in we had been driven towards the wreck of the *Molliette*. This wreck had been a target for gunnery and bombing practice during the Second World War and was a mass of twisted, jagged metal. Through the gloom we could just see the beacon that marked it. I was uneasy with the whole situation as, by now, the wind had risen considerably, along with the sea state, and the anchor warp was surging and sawing itself over the bow roller.

I decided to call for assistance on the VHF radio but that seemed dead, so there was only one thing left to do. We put a rocket up. It seemed like a lifetime but I suppose, in reality, it was about 20 to 30 minutes later that a motor barge in the sand and gravel trade, called the *Peter P*, arrived and I heard her skipper calling on the VHF. Apparently he had heard our calls right from the start but we had not been receiving his replies, which made it obvious that our receiver was faulty at any distance greater than a few hun-dred yards.

Herring net being pulled over the pole with fish on deck and in the hold

He said he would stand by us in case we decided to abandon ship but he would not attempt to come alongside to attach a tow because he felt that the two boats would roll together in the rough sea and cause a lot of damage - mainly to us as the wooden craft. He said that he had received word that the coastguard at Bradwell had asked for the Clacton lifeboat to be launched and she was likely to arrive soon. When she did, it took three attempts to secure a tow warp but, oddly enough, our anchor was hauled with little effort as the lifeboat towed us ahead. We had been prepared to slip it if we were unable to break it out of the ground.

Once round in the direction of the River Colne the motion was much easier as we were running with it. So an uneventful passage was made into Brightlingsea Creek where we moored alongside the fishing vessels opposite the hard. Having made everything secure we rowed ashore to join the lifeboat crew in the Anchor pub for a very welcome drink. The lifeboat was to be left that night in Brightlingsea, to be returned to its station when the weather and the light were more suitable.

It was that evening that I first made the acquaintance of the lifeboat coxswain, Dick Harman, who owned the big Tollesbury stowboat smack *ADC* CK431. Jim Barbrook told me she had been named after three brothers, Albert, Dick and Charlie. During her fishing career she had been cut down to a motor vessel and it was Dick who had re-rigged her in the 1970s.

He told me a nice story that arose out of this re-rigging. It seems that while he was searching for gear he had been told of a mainsail that had been placed with Gowans, the sailmakers at West Mersea, just before the war. The gaff-rigged smacks were having their sails reduced into leg-o-mutton shape because, by this time, the stowboat smacks were becoming motorised with auxillary sails. This sail which had belonged to the *Charlotte Ellen* was never collected because of the outbreak of the war.

Thirty years on, Dick was keen to investigate and made a trip to Gowans where he spoke to a young lad in the sail loft who said he would go and ask. Going into one of the backrooms, the young man enquired of one of the older sailmakers, who then shouted through to Dick: "It ain't ready yet."

In recent times Dick's son Andy has cruised and raced the *ADC* while he himself sails the rebuilt Mersea smack *Electron* CK36.

No words can express properly the sense of relief, safety and comfort we felt as we drank with that most convivial company of lifeboat men.

The next day dawned in an almost totally different world with the sun hanging in a blue sky and boats looking like origami shapes on a glass sea. It made me recall another of the old hands sayings: "Suverly gale soon gawn."

An engineer called Ted Coppin came aboard to look at the seized gearbox. While I stood on deck fearing the worst, he went below, returning not long after with a tiny piece of weed that would have fitted into a teaspoon. It had apparently lodged itself into the oil heat exchanger causing the hydraulic fluid to overheat which led to the seizure. So all Ted had to do was to change the oil and everything was fine. It seemed ridiculous that something so trivial had caused so much bother. And why hadn't the radio worked at the critical moment - it was simply damp.

I even tried changing the boat's name to try and change her luck. I named her *Jayne O*, after a girlfriend, and although it had moderate success it was never the complete answer. As Alan Wright said: "She's a lucky owd bo't. Yer lucky to git orf ut aloive."

He and I discussed the future possibilities of earning a living as a longshoreman and decided that King's theory was nearly right, excepting that a drag for catching mullet would be a profitable addition to the 'drudge iron and pail.'

A short while later Alan found a 16-foot motor launch for sale which we bought for £60 with a Ford Anglia thrown in. We took the engine and gearbox out of the car and Ted Coppin fitted it into the launch, clutch and all. Much later she was to be named *Mayland Oyster* and registered MN13, much against the wishes of the Registrar of Shipping who claimed that no vessel had ever carried this number in the British Isles. Contrary to superstition she was the luckiest boat I have ever been involved with.

The Jayne O - previously known as the Better Hope

Initially though, Alan had christened her 'the big bo't', which gave rise to much amusement because his skiff which had been built for carrying oysters for the Maldon Oyster Company was actually bigger than the launch that towed it. She had so little freeboard that the other fishermen reckoned that we looked like two men on a plank. We used this set-up very profitably for quite some while, trading on oysters, winkles, mullet and bass until Alan decided to sell me his half because he was going to work ashore.

Not for long as it transpired as he soon came back, fitting out a boat called *Lancer* for single-handed use. I owned the *Mayland Oyster* for longer than any other vessel, sometimes at the same time as another. With hindsight I can say that she was the most profitable of all my vessels, mainly because of her lack of overheads. Even though she had a petrol engine, the cost of it was minimal because we were able to claim all the hydrocarbon duty back from the Customs and Excise as she was a registered fishing vessel.

Alan comes from a long line of smacksmen. His father 'Slosha' Jack along with his uncle 'Lucka' worked the family's boat *William* MN15 which had belonged to his grandfather 'Slosha' Bill. When he was in his teens, Alan worked as mate for my father in *Topsy* who recognised him as a born seaman. The worse it became, the better it appeared to suit him. Alan went on from Topsy to become a mate on coastal sailing barges. He worked with 'Pincher' Bloyce in the *Remercie* owned by Horlocks of Mistley.

In later years Pincher was to serve out his times to retirement in the tug, *Lady Barbara*, towing lighters for John Sadd and Sons.

Alan and Pincher once had an argument about whether to make a passage from Harwich to London during some prolonged bad weather. They had been waiting for a fair slant for quite a while. Pincher, who had a family to support and was paid by the freight, was keen to get to London.

Pincher demanded to go.

Alan's reply was based on the fact that he was on a fixed wage as the boy. "Well 'ats loike this. Your ends got the wheel an' yer can take 'ut where yer loike but moi ends got the anchor an' 'ats a stoppin' 'ere."

But the skipper's word is always law and they went.

Alan left the barges and worked a smack called *Dauntless* and then, later, the big smack *Thistle*. She had once been owned and used as a carrier by the Faversham Oyster Company, making weekly trips to the Essex rivers to buy brood oysters from the dredging smacks. While he was skipper of that vessel, she was owned by Mr Pipe who also owned the charter barge *Marjorie*, which sailed from Maldon for several years with Jimmy Lawrence as skipper.

Jim was one of the last true sailormen, as the London dockers called the sailing bargemen. He worked for the Ipswich flour millers, R & W Paul, who kept a fleet of sailing barges going long after sail had disappeared commercially. Because the grain was not needed in any particular hurry, the barges were used as floating warehouses.

Jimmy later became a sailmaker in Brightlingsea, mainly specialising in traditional sails. Alan also had time yachting when he was skipper of Sadd's gaff cutter *Ripple* which chartered from Maldon. Her regular skipper for many years had been 'Daddy' Hedgecock whose failing health resulted in the vessel at some stage or another seeming to have been skippered by just about every waterman in Maldon.

Our first attempt at mullet dragging was not as we had planned it. We had actually gone down the river on a tide that we expected would drop down well, with a view to going 'edging' - picking oysters up. Clive Stebbins from Heybridge Basin was with Alan and I on this occasion. His father, Cecil, owned a boatyard in the village and had been a keen rebuilder of old smacks long before the hobby became popular. Amongst his boats were the *Maud* MN21, once owned by King Wright, the *Ethel Alice* which he had dug out of the mud on Mersea Island and the *Shamrock*. She had been the watch boat for the Tollesbury and West Mersea Native Oyster Company and had been anchored in the mouth of Thirslet Creek carrying out her duties at the start of the 1963 winter when the skim ice formed quickly on the flowing tide, cutting her like a million razor blades until she sank. It was in this state that Cecil bought her for salvage and repaired her.

Clive's grandfather, another Cecil, was at one time the borough council's water bailiff and came from a family of 'hufflers', otherwise known as 'mud pilots', who assisted the coasting barges up the last winding reaches of the Blackwater to Maldon. Grandfather Cecil was, in fact, employed by Trinity House as the Sunk pilot for the Blackwater and brought many sizeable ships into the town.

The Wright's boat, William, with Slosha, Alan, Lucka, Emmie and Ken Ridgewell aboard

In his early days he was part of a delivery crew working for May and Butcher, the shipbreakers at Heybridge Basin. They were bringing a first ship of the line, called *Marlborough*, under tow from Portsmouth to the Blackwater in 1924. The ship met her fate at The Nabb at the eastern end of the Solent, by sinking rather than at the hands of the wreckers at the Basin. Cecil and Jim Stebbins were the only two survivors out of the entire crew.

Another ship worthy of mention is the *Astrid Gloriana*, an American windjammer which had broken her back on her maiden voyage across the Atlantic. She then became a store ship at Rowhedge and was then purchased by May and Butcher to be used as a store at the Basin, holding scrap metal taken from broken ships which was then exported to Germany in the 1930s. 'Young' Cecil told me: "It was alright, though. Hitler, being fair, re-exported it to us in the 1940s in the form of bombs."

The *Gloria* met her own fate, when she was consumed by fire in 1937. The story has it that she burnt for a week and the heat was so intense that it was feared that the houses around the Basin would catch fire as well. The aft-deckhouse of the ship still survives and is in used as an outbuilding in Wharf Road, Millbeach.

But back to the mullet fishing. While we were waiting for the last of the tide to ebb away, we noticed fish swimming around us and, as luck would have it, we had the drag in the stern sheets of the skiff. We made two shots, filling Alan's massive skiff up to the thwarts with a mixture of mullet and bass. This time we were in the right place at the right time with the right gear.

More often the net would be laid out and then the search for fish would begin, travelling sometimes miles in and out of creeks and investigating various spits until fish were seen to move. Mullet jump, a bit like salmon, or turn and leave a whirlpool in the water. An indication to where they had been feeding on the previous tide were the marks they left on the mud, made when their split lips and under fins touched the mud. The marks look as if somebody has drawn two fingers, slightly apart, across the surface for about two to three inches.

The net for mullet is similar to a herring net in that it is a sheet of netting, but that is where the resemblance ends. The 150 yards of continual netting with a three inch mesh has a head line with corks and a heavy leaded line 12 feet below it.

The gear is shot in a semi-circle. Starting from the water's edge or 'cant', it is rowed out and back and the net is then pulled ashore. I found mullet dragging a most exhilarating job because you are in close contact with the fish. It becomes a contest between you and them - and sometimes they won.

We were working in the shoals at Millbeach one night when so many fish hit the downriver wing, it could not be held. The shoal took the net out into deeper water where they were able to escape. It was an amazing sight to see several yards of net rise out of the water with jumping fish.

When Alan left, my relation Keith Yuille came in to fill the mate's position. Our family connection was through the Croziers from Chapel Lane, Heybridge Basin. The Basin had been nicknamed Cannibal Island for years - probably because it was a tiny close-knit, almost mystic, community. Our third hand was a chap from Steeple Stone known as 'Dave the Grave', owing to the fact that he was always digging holes in the beach looking for lugworms.

We practised dragging to great effect that year but recognised that the job only had a limited amount of time in which it could be carried out because of the need to have a water's edge to which the net could be pulled. We also noticed that the largest shoals of fish were not coming onto the mud or into the creeks until everywhere was underwater. The answer to this came when we purchased some mono-filament gill nets which could be anchored in these shallows in the path of the mullet. Apart from a short thin period in July, mullet fishing went on right through the summer into the autumn. In fact, the best fishing was generally in the autumn when the fish shoaled more and spent more time feeding in the shallows.

Crewing the boats was generally a matter of family first and then only when the trade could support them or actually required the men to work together. For instance, winkling was a job that made more economic sense when a man worked on his own. So although three men - or considerably more - might crew a smack for dredging, they would work separately winkling until dragging time came around. The nature of the job required several hands and so they would get back together, even taking on others just for that time. It was this pool type of work alliance that led me to work with 'Young' Ted Pitt on the *Ann* MN24 for a short while when I first turned professional.

Ted had previously worked with his father since he had left school, both in the *Ann* and in the fast little smack *Fly* MN17. 'Old' Ted had bought the *Fly* from Ipswich at a cost of £75 which I am told upset his wife considerably because he had spent every last halfpenny they had got.

John Sadd's Ripple

Although the boat was registered *Fly* when he bought her, Ted told me that the name carved under the counter was *Violet Bella* which was probably her original name when she was built. She sported a very long fine counter which, although it looked pretty, was a source of annoyance when anchored with a sea running. Having spent a very uncomfortable night with the counter slamming badly, Ted took the boat home to Maldon where he made his first job sawing it off. He replaced it with a form of transom, vowing that it would never keep him awake again. His father had owned the smacks *Phantom, Ethel* and *Fashion*.

Ted's yachting career was served in the large gentleman's yacht *Vanity*, kept at Burnham-on-Crouch. His departure from fishing was, to say the least, abrupt. He appeared on the Bath Wall one morning, bag in hand as if to go to work as normal, had a few words with King Wright, declared that he was retired and that the boat was Young Teds' responsibility now and that King would be his crew.

My involvement with Ted came because King decided that he wanted to work alone picking winkles. This enabled him to please himself which days he worked as he, too, by this time was drawing his pension. The boat again supplied the family with employment in latter years when Ted's son, David, joined him after leaving school.

Old Ted once had one of the oddest jobs in the industry - catching goldfish out of the ornamental lake which fronts Boreham House, now Ford's International Training Centre. He built a drag especially for the job and told me that he received half a crown for every one that he could keep alive.

Much later he was to sell me this net and also the large saltwater drag which we used for catching eels. An eel drag varied in length and depth depending on whether it was to be used in the salt estuary or in the brackish delphs and freshwater fleets. The big net when it was wet took two men to lift it and when it was shot in a tideway it needed a pulling effort which sometimes seemed beyond us.

At the time I bought these nets, I was working with Kingy on and off and actually had bought them at his suggestion. It was my belief that eel dragging was his favourite job. I not only learnt a great deal from him but also enjoyed the time that I worked with him because he was an extremely jovial character and had a wealth of stories which gave us many hearty laughs. As I look back now, I feel that I was almost apprenticed to him, rather like the old institution of the boy being apprecticed to a craftsman, for although I was not being directly taught, just being in company of someone with great knowledge makes for a situation where a little must rub off.

His vast store of knowledge about sailing vessels and fishing came from a lifetime of being in smacks and barges. Just a few of his involvements were with his father in the *Maud* MN 21, with 'Hobby' Keeble in the sailing barge *Dawn*, with 'Skatey' Dick and 'Care' Wright in the *Lizzy Annie* MN23 and eel fishing on the Norfolk Broads with Arther Rice.

One of his stories from the barging era was the bizarre sight in Maldon of a sailing barge sitting half on the quay and half in the river at Maldon with her mast describing an angle of 45 degrees. She was found in this predicament on the morning of the 7th January 1928 by her skipper Billy 'Bundick' Austin.

The previous night's tide is still the biggest on record, beating even the famous flood of February 1953. King and Hobby were waiting with the *Dawn* for a freight at Felixstowe. Waking in the middle of the night and taking the habitual look out of the hatch, all King could see was the rounded tops of the railway carriages on the dockside and a whole row of floating beach huts that had made their way round to the dock from the other side of the headland on the flood tide.

The wind the previous day had been a severe northerly gale which had created the tidal phenomenon. When the tide came that night it was with a dead flat calm which is the main reason why the barge *Mermaid* ended up at that precarious angle on the quay. Everbody assumed that because the wind had dropped, everything would be alright. Billy Austin, who had been one of my grandfather's skippers in earlier days, worked the *Mermaid* for Jimmy Last, the builders' merchant. She had brought a freight of cement and chalk from Kent which she had discharged in the Heybridge yard. To reach the yard she had been taken up Heybridge Creek and under the black bridge of the Causeway with her gear lowered. She had returned, light, back to the Hythe to lie awaiting orders. Her odd berth did not seem to hurt the barge too much, as she was easily relaunched with the aid of greasyways and the next flood tide and she went on to take the winner's pennant in the 1929 Maldon Barge Match.

One of Billy's much later commands was the *Ethel Maud* which he traded for Greens, the flour millers of Maldon.

From the many stories of King Wright's fishing career, I remember his description of a wild and rainy night that he spent in Norfolk with Arthur Rice who actually came from Acle. He owned a boom net for catching eels running between the Broads. This net had similarities to the stow boat net used for catching sprats in that it had a square mouth which could be closed by pulling the bottom to the top enclosing the catch in a funnel resembling a trawl. But the sprat net has wooden beams while the boom net had a wire at the head and a heavy chain on the bottom, both of which were pulled across the dyke by a hand winch. With the wire on the surface and the chain on the bottom everything that swam down the dyke had to pass into the net.

One night torrential rain and high winds caused almost flood conditions and Kingy was concerned for his own safety because he was afraid that the

The barge Mermaid in an uncomfortable berth on the Hythe following the big tide of January 7 1928. Thistle and Grace Darling are in the foreground

shed he was sheltering in alongside the net would be swept away. His answer, for peace of mind, was to tie the shed to the nearest tree with a rope passing right around it.

When dawn broke it was obvious that he was safe but he could see his next problem. The flood waters had brought so many eels down the dyke that the massive boom net was like a huge silver writhing sausage. His problem was how to discharge the net until he remembered the words of a very old Norfolk eelman who had had to deal with this problem in the past and had explained the answer to him. The eels were to be kept in a large floating trunk and the problem was to transfer the eels from the net to the trunk when there was absolutely no way of lifting the net.

He undid the pod, the exit end of the net, and lowered this into the top of the trunk. Then he stood in the trunk himself, making it sink slightly. Eels, by nature, go with the flow of the water and always look for an escape route from the position they are in, so they followed each other almost nose to tail - elephant fashion - out of the net and into the trunk. Not a single eel out of this mammoth catch had escaped by the time the lid of the trunk was pegged down.

The drag net used for eels was similar to a mullet drag but it was made from very much smaller mesh netting. The wings were $3/4$ inch and the cod was $3/8$ inch. It differed from the mullet net in that it had a cod end with a tunnel stitched inside it to prevent the eels from running back and escaping. It was shot out of a skiff in the same way, except that it had to be laid in the stern sheet the correct way to ensure that the cod was on the outside of the semi-circle. A piece of coloured twine was put on the end of the wing that would be first into the skiff, for shooting the ebb tide on the Millbeach side, thus showing which end to deal with.

I got to know Andrew Woodhead, a farm manager who worked for Strutt and Parker, who lived in one of their farmhouses at Dammerwick on Burnham Marshes alongside a large freshwater reservoir used for irrigating the potato crop. He gave us permission to fish this water and King and I used to take a dinghy on a trailer to use the large drag for catching the eels which had been a nuisance to Andrew, blocking his pumps regularly.

We did reasonably well on odd occasions, but the one night that sticks out in my memory was not because of the catch but because we were eaten alive by gnats. I complained but King said: "We'll be alright in a minute."

Looking along his outstretched arm to where he was pointing, I saw a black line emerging from the roof of a derelict farmhouse. Within seconds we were surrounded by bats who only took a few minutes to clear the air of every insect.

Eels caught in freshwater always seem to be a lot livelier than those from the salt. Before they were shipped to the market, eels from the fresh had to be 'swum', that is held in trunks in the salt water which made them disgorge any food, thus stabilizing their weight and preventing them from choking in transit. One of our best customers was Bob Cooke, a man from a family who for generations past owned and ran eel, pie and mash shops in the East End of London.

Eels are most resourceful creatures and are a complete study in them-selves. Some of their behaviour is still not understood by man.

Ged Wright once told me that he had been with his uncles in the *Harriet Blanche* MN42 when her skipper, 'Emma', who was regarded as one of the best eel fishermen in Maldon decided to take the large drag and a punt over the seawall into the fleet at Stansgate, known as the Wade.

This fleet had been created many, many years before by Dutch engi-neers who had dammed off what had been the creek that circumnavigated Ramsey Island on which stands Stee-ple Stone. This now brackish lake was a good spot for eel fishing which is always carried out in the pitch black, preferably with the wind from the south west and a little 'mizzle' of rain. A northerly wind 'puts the eels to bed.'

The pilot vessel Patricia with Old Cecil Stebbings being rowed aboard a vessel bound for the Blackwater

On this occasion the conditions were perfect but the net shot round to produce a complete blank and a second shot produced the same. Some-what bewildered, the crew decided to return to the warmth of the cabin to consider what they had got wrong. On the journey from the fleet back to the seawall somebody dropped something and, as the use of artifical light by this time no longer mattered, the torch was switched on in the search. It was then that the answer to the empty net became evident. The eels were actually making their way in their hundreds over the damp grass towards the seawall in order to return to the river. Needless to say the rest of the night was spent chasing eels and collecting them up into purse nets.

During dry periods, the Wade water level dropped below that necessary to float the net properly and on these occasions a tiny pebble would be lodged behind the sluice gate allowing salt water from the river to enter the fleet.

Ged told me that when he was a lad his uncles had told him to carry out this minor operation but in his enthusiasm and not realising the force of the water, he had put a brick behind the gate. All was going well until the men with the net realised that this normally still water was actually taking the wings of the net landward with as much ferocity as the movement of the tide of the river. Some concern was felt that they might return Ramsey Island to its former glory and Ged was given some lessons in the sizes of pebbles.

Gleaning a living from any form of fishing is a precarious business because you really are only as good as your last trip. Blank times, gear losses and fickle markets meant that there was no such thing as an ordinary day's work because you never knew when the work would evaporate or when the next opportunity would arise. So the pace of work on a good day would be as if it were the last for some time - even if it were not.

The blank times or days of bad weather were called 'days to the King' -the royal variety in this case - and they bred philosophical, eternally optimistic characters. To quote Kingy just once more: "Something will always come along if you can afford to wait long enough."

THE END AND THE PHOENIX

V ery few smacks were built after 1900 so by the time I started fishing they were all very old. This, combined with the fact that little was spent on proper structural replacement when a botch to get by was the order of the day, meant that a lot of the boats were in an awful state. The old hands were not be blamed for this attitude, though, because they were all ageing themselves and, with next to none of their sons taking to the job, they only required 'the bo'ts to see us out.'

My friend Alan said to me one day: "Oi've come to see the mayfloats."

I though there must be a carnival or fete on but when I asked what he meant he replied: "They may float, they may not."

The old hands had been saying since long before I started: "It will all come to a round O" and that the smacks would disappear.

Their prediction has come true in so far as the smacks no longer work in the time honoured fashion, nor does anybody gain their livelihood in the manner they did. By the mid to late Seventies earning a living from the old established ways was impossible, but earnings from the river were kept going for a few years by the development of the oyster layings, run by individuals under leases from Maldon District Council.

Most of the old hands had sadly disappeared by this time and not one working smack was left. The trade was carried out by about ten men in a variety of motor dredgers which carried a single dredge ranging from four to five feet across the scythe and it was pulled up mechanically. The culch was landed on a table, which was built to sit on the top of the bulwarks so that the unwanted material could be simply pushed overboard. The old accepted patterns of tide and wind hardly applied any more.

Overleaf: Ted Pitt and his son, David, in the Ann mooring up after a day's power dredging in 1979

The boat that I owned by this time was a French shrimper built in Gravelines, *Notre Dame des Dunes* CK239. She was nicknamed the oil rig because of her mass of steel pipe rigging used for power dredging and stern trawling - a very different creature from the traditional smack.

Her engine and winch gear were so powerful that they could pull the boat right over if the gear was tight on a 'fastener' - caught on an obstruction. With diving plates on the dredges and because they no longer had to be hauled hand over hand, much deeper water and stronger tides could be worked. In fact, the power dredge actually worked better on the hard flood, a time when hand dredgers could not hold the bottom. The tipping out of the dredge net was even modernised by the introduction of a rigid frame in which to put the ring hide and net. This was held closed by a hook arrangement which would be tripped by a handle, allowing the material to fall onto the table from the dredge which would be suspended from above by a derrick.

One excursion we did have with the *Notre Dame* was on a tide that we expected to ebb well out. We anchored her in the mouth of the swatch which leads to the Back of The Maine with the intention of going edging for oysters. The tide was extraordinary with the ebb much further out than even we had anticipated, revealing wrecks of aeroplanes and all manner of other junk, making us wonder how we ever steered clear while trawling that area.

One particular wreck, I was told by my cousin who was into that sort of thing, was a Dornier which still had propellers sticking up off one engine although both wings had been severed from the fuselage, probably by the impact when it hit the sea. We removed one of the machine guns and my cousin, who was a member of the Essex Aviation Group, sent the gun to the Imperial War Museum at Duxford.

Reports came back that a round was actually travelling down the barrel of the gun at the moment of impact and was stopped half way. Although the gun had been in the water for 35 years, after a short while in their workshop they managed to get the mechanism to operate.

Although the idea of growing oysters on to full ware instead of selling them as half ware and brood was helping the economics of the job, the marketing still involved the merchants of West Mersea. This meant that we were at the bottom of the profit chain and survival required that we moved up and become merchants ourselves.

This led to the establishment of a new firm, the Maldon Oyster Fishery. We were able then to sell our own oysters direct and achieve the maximum income from them. In the first two seasons bulk loads were exported to a Dutch buyer, Rinus Verwys of Laundeur International in Yerseke. But in the third season the exchange rate made it uneconomical to export so we had to turn to the home market which had already reached saturation point of supply.

A sample was sent to Wheelers Restaurants in the West End and Wiltons of St James's who both liked the quality and placed orders, becoming regular customers. This must be testament to the quality of the oysters grown at the top end of the Blackwater as we were able to find orders in that climate.

Billingsgate Market was also used, when it was at its original site in Fish Street and Lower Thames Street near the Tower of London. Bloomfields and John Lipscomb's became regular market customers, with Lipscomb's exporting oysters as far as the Middle East.

The need for co-operation in the new climate showed with the setting up of the Maldon Oyster Fisherman's Association to deal with matters regarding the fishery which were discussed at twice yearly meetings with the district council. So the trade had taken on a business face, with purification certificates, meetings, invoices, packaging and van deliveries - a far cry from the simple days of the smacksmen.

But an abrupt end came to the oyster industry as a whole in the early 1980s. A disease, bonamia, had unfortunately been transmitted by natural movement of stock in trade from abroad to the river Fal in Cornwall and later to West Mersea. Although the Maldon grounds were not directly affected, a directive was received from the Ministry of Agriculture, Fisheries and Food to curtail production and lay the grounds fallow in an attempt to halt the spread of the disease.

Tommy Pitt's Letitia power dredging. His son Chris is at the winch

This extreme measure was taken mainly because little research had been done and little knowledge existed about the nature of the disease and how it was transmitted. But it really was the final nail in the coffin of the industry because the natural stock on the main fishery had already been badly depleted by overdredging a stock that had not seen a significant spat-fall since 1976. Excessive bait digging, more moorings and ever in-

creasing pollution were evident in their effect, not only on oysters but on every other species that used to inhabit or grow in the river.

One by one my associates at the Maldon end of the river left fishing and in October 1985 I became the last to concede, carrying in my mind what the old hand had said: "It'll come to a round 0."

About half way through the life of the Maldon Oyster Fishery I decided to sell my French stern trawler in favour of building a smack. The writing by this time was on the wall and the only commercial work left was dredging on oyster layings. The trawler was totally unsuitable for this work for she was much too powerful and drew too much water. Catching oysters almost in the old gentlemanly way, with small gear, made it obvious to me that a smack was the vessel for the job. Also, a use for the boat when the commercial work was finished was a prime consideration and, therefore, a vessel that could be rigged for sailing had to be the choice.

Having looked around for a second hand vessel, I found that they were either owned by people who were not interested in selling or that the smacks were in such bad order that they would have been total rebuilds. So I started considering a brand new boat.

The statement that finally clinched the matter came from 'Sonny' Cardy as I stood talking to him on the Hythe one day in 1979.

Notre Dames des Dunes de Gravelines - 'the oil rig'

"That's about time you stopped playing around with those old boats and 'ad a new one," he said.

Sonny was, amongst other things, the one time skipper of the pleasure craft *Viking Saga* which traded from the extension on Maldon Promenade. His wife Rene, supplied the entertainment to their passengers with her piano accordion. After she left Maldon the *Viking* worked from Clacton for a while.

My new boat, *Ostrea Rose* MN183 was launched at Heybridge Basin on August Bank Holiday 1980, rigged as a motor driven power dredger. Her design was largely based on the boats that my great great grandfather had had built in the 1880s. So, with certain additions and refinements which I had seen in many other vessels, she is basically a bawley although she carries a boom in the fashion of the oyster boats, perpetuating the refinement that the 'owd man' made. Her name *Ostrea* comes from the Latin and means oyster, which is what she caught up until the demise of the industry.

Opposite: the more attractive lines of Ostrea Rose in the River Orwell in 1991

After that fateful time a long laid up period ensued during which time I removed her winch gear, fitted out the accommodation below decks and rigged her with the traditional smack's gaff cutter rig.

When I was searching for gear I made a trip to a long established riggers at Burnham where I found two elderly employees. I told them I was looking for wooden blocks, bullseyes, hooks and the like and they asked me what they were intended for. When I told them I was fitting out a new smack, they remarked that they had not fitted out one in Burnham since before the war.

I told them I was from Maldon and they said that one of the Maldon smacksmen used to crew on one of the big yachts they had both worked on. "Yes," I said. "Ted Pitt, who used to work in the *Vanity*."

The two men seemed surprised that I knew Ted and were delighted when I said that I not only knew him but that I had worked with his son in the *Ann* after his retirement.

This little bit of name dropping stood me well, for it seemed that I could almost have had the entire shed for ten bob and left with two boxes of very fine gear, being told to get out quick "before the guv'nor comes back." Other gear came from one of my oyster suppliers, Derek Leavett, who let me have the blocks that had been in his father's smack. The *lignum vitae* dead-eyes, which were of ancient origin, came from the sailmaker Jimmy Lawrence. All of this gave the new boat an antique patina which has fooled the most discerning eye. On one occasion a chap asked how old she was, to which I replied: "She's six."

"What one hundred and six?"

"No six," I said.

But he still would not believe me and went away saying: "They don't build boats like that these days."

Having rigged her out I then worked ashore for three years rebuilding a 17th century timber framed house but the magnet which draws men to salt water was inflicting its power by then.

This was so great a pull that I decided to again eke out a precarious living from the sea. History was again going full circle and I became a yacht charterer as my father had been.

Maldon Smack Race winners 1960. Left to right, Stan South, Bill 'Belty' Sexton, Dick Wright and Mr and Mrs John Kemp

Opposite: Dick Wright on board Lizzie Annie. She is now rebuilt and sailing far beyond her original waters

Whilst I lament those magical days of my boyhood when boats names and exploits were synonymous with family names that had histories stretching back centuries, it is heart warming to visit the races and regattas now to see a fleet of smacks which have been entirely rebuilt for and by enthusiastic amateurs.

One of these amateurs who can be called the ultimate enthusiast is Richard Titchener who, along with the Maldon based shipwright Brian Kennel, saved the second class smack *Sallie* ex MN39 from death on a corporation rubbish tip at Whitby in Yorkshire. Reports of the old lady's plight had reached Brian who then with Richard visited her. They decided that they would temporarily patch her up and float her to a nearby wharf where she could be loaded by crane onto a trailer. The haulier Arthur Keeble then transported her to the Downs Road Boatyard in Maldon, where both he and Brian are two of the partners.

Initially they decided to replace the very bad structural timbers and retain the not so bad. With this in mind they replaced the keel and the lower frames but by then it was becoming more and more apparent that she needed a lot more work than they had at first thought. Brian decided that the project would need substantial finance in order to succeed and that because of other commitments - not the least of which was his own smack *Hyacinth* CK256 - he would not be able to supply it.

Richard then took the bull by the horns, taking on the whole project. Having bought Brian's share from him he remortgaged his house and not only employed Brian but also Ian Danskin, Jamie Clay, Fabian Bush and a young Dutch girl call Jan at various times during her eight year rebuild. Having sailed aboard her I can say that it was well worth all the effort for she is a handy vessel and top competition at the smack races.

Another keen racing man is Bob Fawkes who rebuilt the fast little smack *Lizzie Annie* MN23 in his back garden next door to the White Horse at Mundon. Her speed was illustrated to me when Kingy told me that while he was working in her with Dick and 'Care' they actually swung flood at Fambridge on Burnham river and were able to save that high water to Maldon. A good southerly did help.

One of Bob's first sails in *Lizzie* before her rebuild was the sad honour of spreading ashes on the water, following the death of one of her former owners, Dick Wright.

Although *Lizzie* was only built for work in the rivers, Bob's adventurous nature has taken her much further. Just one occasion was when he crossed to the Atlantic coast of France where she attended the Chasse Maree Festival at Dourenenez in 1988.

Out of all the rebuild projects, one worthy of mention must be *Nellie*, which was completely fashioned by the owners, John Bissel and Maureen.

In fact, after the hull was complete, on which Maureen undertook the intricate work of pattern making and fitting, she then on her own designed and fitted out the interior, banning John from the job. They have kept the deck layout original with whole hatches and a tiny scuttle hatch for the cabin, so that her original owners, the Vince family of oystermen from West Mersea, would instantly recognise her.

The Vinces had her built by Walter Cook and Son at Maldon in 1888 and worked her until the outbreak of the Second World War in 1939. After the war she was sold to be converted to a yacht.

I saw her at Burnham in the 1970s where she was used as a tug, by which time she had had her counter cut off and replaced with a transom. She also had a wheelhouse and a funnel, leaving the only clue to her original identity in the bow roller and gammon iron, typical of a smack. After this she deteriorated and was left to sink near Rice and Coles' boatyard, from where she was purchased and taken to Heybridge Basin, where she was again abandoned. John bought her for 64p as a half-tide wreck. This purchase price was chosen for luck as it happened not only to coincide with a price of one pence per share - for these boats were traditionally owned by 64/64th shares - but also because it was the price of a pint of Greene King bitter at the time.

Tollesbury Regatta 1989. The author with Ostrea Rose and Electron sailing close behind

These boats and many others can be seen practically every weekend and some whole weeks in the summer months, racing on the East Coast rivers at such events as the now hugely popular Old Gaffers' Race, held on the Blackwater. Mersea Town Regatta has its traditional element and the Colchester Oyster Fishery Race still has as part of the course an element recalling the working days of the boats when they have to catch an oyster under sail.

There are also the annual trips south to do battle with the Kentish men, when the smacks of the Colne and Blackwater meet the bawleys of the Medway and the Swale. So, at least the spectacle of the tan sails is maintained even if their commercial role has gone, along with those professional smacksmen and sailormen whom I hold in great affection and who now, in the main, rest in more peaceful anchorages.

Overleaf: Maldon sunset

GLOSSARY

BACCA - JUICE	*plankton bloom (very bad for clogging nets)*
BLONDS	*prime skate.*
BOB	*flag.*
BO'LIN	*piece of line on the foreward shroud used to hold the staysail a'weather.*
BOWER	*smacks main anchor.*
BRACKISH	*semi-saline water, normally found in the dykes inside the seawalls.*
BRING UP	*to come to anchor.*
BROWN EEL	*eel before it has been into the fresh water.*
CAMP SHED	*wooden cladding to the seawalls.*
CATS PAWS	*wisps of breeze on the water on calm days.*
CHAIN OF MESHES	*the start of making a net.*
CLEANT	*to have scrubbed off the bottom of the boat or to have washed it out.*
CLOCK	*empty shell of an oyster, lately died but still joined at the hinge.*
DAG	*dew.*
DIRT	*weed caught in a net.*
DOORMATS	*very large soles.*
DRIVE	*a boat drifting with the tide.*
FLEET	*an inland lake or a term used meaning to come afloat.*
FRANK	*nick name for a heron.*
FROTH	*bubbly substance which forms at low water and hails the flood tide.*
GRASS	*eel grass (zostrea)*
GUT STARVING WIND	*north easterly wind.*
HODNIDODS	*very large winkles*
INK FISH	*cuttle fish.*
LET-GO	*to drop anchor.*
LUST	*to lay the boat over on one side when aground.*
LARNCH	*to drag a small boat across the ground.*
MAID	*a small skate or roker.*
NUNS	*barnacles.*
PAINTER	*rope for tying up the bow of a skiff.*
PAN-WAYS	*indentations in the mud retaining water.*
PRIME	*choice fish.*
RILL	*small creek in the saltings.*
ROKER	*thorn back ray (skate family)*
ROPEWAYS	*positions on the gunwales where thole pins are placed to retain oars while rowing.*
SANDBACKS	*flounders with a sandy colour instead of being white.*
SCRIMMAGE	*line of froth running up the middle of the channel on the flood tide when it is reasonably calm. A good navigational aid when foggy.*

NET & TACKLE

HAND HAULED OYSTER DREDGE

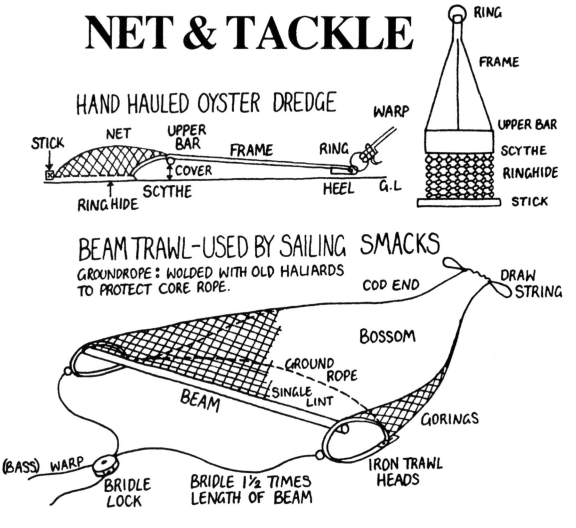

STICK
NET
UPPER BAR
FRAME
RING
WARP
COVER
SCYTHE
RING HIDE
HEEL
G.L

RING
FRAME
UPPER BAR
SCYTHE
RINGHIDE
STICK

BEAM TRAWL—USED BY SAILING SMACKS

GROUNDROPE: WOLDED WITH OLD HALIARDS
TO PROTECT CORE ROPE.

COD END
DRAW STRING
BOSSOM
GROUND ROPE
BEAM
SINGLE LINT
GORINGS
(BASS) WARP
BRIDLE LOCK
BRIDLE 1½ TIMES
LENGTH OF BEAM
IRON TRAWL HEADS

OTTER TRAWL—USED BY MOTOR FISHING VESSELS

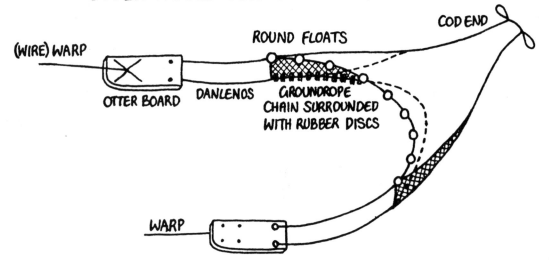

(WIRE) WARP
ROUND FLOATS
COD END
OTTER BOARD
DANLENOS
GROUNDROPE
CHAIN SURROUNDED
WITH RUBBER DISCS
WARP

HERRING DRIFT NET

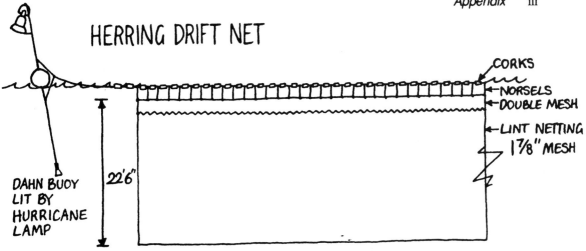

THE DAHN BUOYS, LIT BY HURRICANE LAMPS, WERE TO MARK BOTH ENDS OF THE GEAR. EACH NET WAS 35 YARDS LONG AND WERE JOINED TOGETHER TO ACHEIVE THE LENGTH REQUIRED TO FISH.

MULLET DRAG — BEACH SEINE

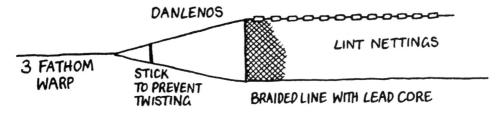

TWO MEN HAUL NET TO SHORE, WORKING CLOSER TOGETHER AS NET COMES IN, LEAVING WINGS LAYING AT N.E THE BUNT WITH FISH IN, IS GROUNDED IN MIDDLE.

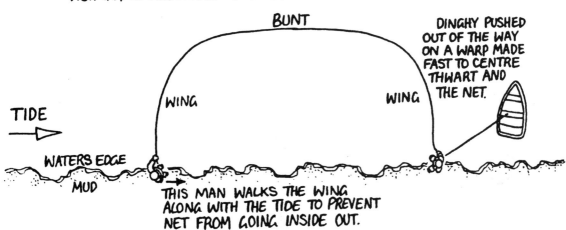

PETER NET

SIDE VIEW

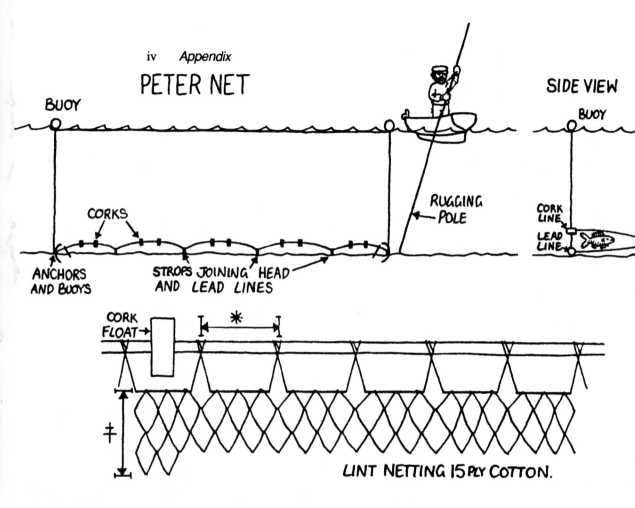

BUOY

CORKS

ANCHORS
AND BUOYS

STROPS JOINING HEAD
AND LEAD LINES

RUGGING
POLE

BUOY

CORK
LINE

LEAD
LINE

CORK
FLOAT

LINT NETTING 15 PLY COTTON.

SUSPENDING BOTH HEAD AND LEAD LINES TOGETHER, THE NET WAS JOINED
BY USING 30 PLY COTTON, MADE FAST WITH ROLLING HITCHES AROUND
THE ROPES. WORKING ON BOTH LINES AT THE SAME TIME INSURED
THAT THEY WERE LEVEL. EACH DIVISION ✱ WAS CALLED A "YORKEN"
AND MEASURED TWO STRETCHED MESHES ‡ ALONG AND THREE
FINGERS IN DEPTH. THE FIRST ROW OF MESHES WERE DOUBLE TWINE
AND WAS CALLED "SALVAGED". THE STROPS WERE MADE OF 32 PLY
AND VARIED IN LENGTH DEPENDING UPON WHAT THE USE OF THE
NET WAS TO BE.
FLOUNDERS REQUIRED ABOUT 4" WHILST ROKER (SKATE) LENGTHENED
TO BETWEEN 9"-12". TO COMPLETE THE BAG EFFECT EACH END OF
THE LINT WAS LACED ABOUT TWO THIRDS OF THE WAY UP TO THE
LINES. THE WEIGHTS ON THE BOTTOM LINE WERE CUT FROM SHEET
LEAD AND DRESSED AROUND THE LINE. WITH SLIGHT VARIATIONS,
DEPENDING ON THE USE A NET WAS TO BE PUT TO, ALL GEAR WAS
BUILT IN THIS FASHION.

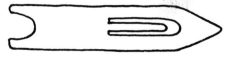

NETTING NEEDLE SIZE VARIED
ACCORDING TO MESH SIZE

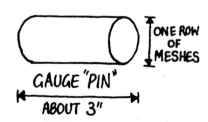

ONE ROW
OF
MESHES

GAUGE "PIN"

ABOUT 3"